JF
1411
L43
1999

NEW DIRECTIONS FOR EVALUATION
A Publication of the American Evaluation Association

Gary T. Henry, *Georgia State University*
COEDITOR-IN-CHIEF

Jennifer C. Greene, *Cornell University*
COEDITOR-IN-CHIEF

Legislative Program Evaluation: Utilization-Driven Research for Decision Makers

R. Kirk Jonas
University of Richmond

EDITOR

Number 81, Spring 1999

JOSSEY-BASS PUBLISHERS
San Francisco

LEGISLATIVE PROGRAM EVALUATION: UTILIZATION-DRIVEN RESEARCH FOR
DECISION MAKERS
R. Kirk Jonas (ed.)
New Directions for Evaluation, no. 81
Jennifer C. Greene, Gary T. Henry, Coeditors-in-Chief

Microfilm copies of issues and articles are available in 16mm and 35mm,
as well as microfiche in 105mm, through University Microfilms Inc., 300
North Zeeb Road, Ann Arbor, Michigan 48106-1346.

New Directions for Evaluation is indexed in Contents Pages in Education,
Higher Education Abstracts, and Sociological Abstracts.

ISSN 1097-6736   ISBN 0-7879-4901-9

NEW DIRECTIONS FOR EVALUATION is part of The Jossey-Bass Education
Series and is published quarterly by Jossey-Bass Inc., Publishers, 350 Sansome Street, San Francisco, California 94104–1342.

SUBSCRIPTIONS cost $65.00 for individuals and $115.00 for institutions,
agencies, and libraries. Prices subject to change.

EDITORIAL CORRESPONDENCE should be addressed to the Coeditors-in-
Chief, Jennifer C. Greene, Department of Policy Analysis and Management,
MVR Hall, Cornell University, Ithaca, NY 14853-4401, or Gary T. Henry,
School of Policy Studies, Georgia State University, P.O. Box 4039, Atlanta,
GA 30302-4039.

Cover design by Design Office.

www.josseybass.com

Printed in the United States of America on acid-free recycled paper con-
taining 100 percent recovered waste paper, of which at least 20 percent is
postconsumer waste.

EDITORIAL POLICY AND PROCEDURES

New Directions for Evaluation, a quarterly sourcebook, is an official publication of the American Evaluation Association. The journal publishes empirical, methodological, and theoretical works on all aspects of evaluation. A reflective approach to evaluation is an essential strand to be woven through every volume. The editors encourage volumes that have one of three foci: (1) craft volumes that present approaches, methods, or techniques that can be applied in evaluation practice, such as the use of templates, case studies, or survey research; (2) professional issue volumes that present issues of import for the field of evaluation, such as utilization of evaluation or locus of evaluation capacity; (3) societal issue volumes that draw out the implications of intellectual, social, or cultural developments for the field of evaluation, such as the women's movement, communitarianism, or multiculturalism. A wide range of substantive domains is appropriate for New Directions for Evaluation; however, the domains must be of interest to a large audience within the field of evaluation. We encourage a diversity of perspectives and experiences within each volume, as well as creative bridges between evaluation and other sectors of our collective lives.

The editors do not consider or publish unsolicited single manuscripts. Each issue of the journal is devoted to a single topic, with contributions solicited, organized, reviewed, and edited by a guest editor. Issues may take any of several forms, such as a series of related chapters, a debate, or a long article followed by brief critical commentaries. In all cases, the proposals must follow a specific format, which can be obtained from the editor-in-chief. These proposals are sent to members of the editorial board and to relevant substantive experts for peer review. The process may result in acceptance, a recommendation to revise and resubmit, or rejection. However, the editors are committed to working constructively with potential guest editors to help them develop acceptable proposals.

Jennifer C. Greene, Coeditor-in-Chief
Department of Policy Analysis and Management
MVR Hall
Cornell University
Ithaca, NY 14853–4401
e-mail: jcg8@cornell.edu

Gary T. Henry, Coeditor-in-Chief
School of Policy Studies
Georgia State University
P.O. Box 4039
Atlanta, GA 30302–4039
e-mail: gthenry@gsu.edu

CONTENTS

EDITOR'S NOTES

The genesis for this project began well before my involvement with it. For a number of years, practitioners in the field of legislative program evaluation (LPE) have discussed the notion that their work is at once part of, and yet somehow distinct from, the overall field of program evaluation. Out of these discussions came a general desire to familiarize the wider evaluation community with legislative program evaluation. The "pracademics" (practitioner-academics) among us thought that the New Directions for Evaluation series would be a perfect vehicle for this purpose. The executive committee of the National Legislative Program Evaluation Society (NLPES, a staff section of the National Conference of State Legislatures) endorsed the project and promoted the participation of its membership.

With encouragement from Gary Henry, at that time a member of the advisory board and later a New Directions coeditor, the project began to move forward. His "pracademic" background included a stint in legislative program evaluation, and he was familiar with—and appreciative of—the place of LPE within the wider evaluation community. After what I expect are some of the usual fits and starts, this volume came together.

Legislative program evaluation is justifiably obsessed with utilization. Simply stated, legislatures commission evaluations they expect to use. Further, legislators expect evaluation results that are timely, sensible, and comprehensible. Such expectations are not unreasonable. Legislators are, after all, the customer.

It is the evaluators themselves who sometimes complicate matters. Coming from auditing, academic, evaluation, and other professional backgrounds, the evaluators realize that the probability of utilization raises the stakes. Reports that are going to be used must meet a high standard of rigor. Of course, they must also be timely, sensible, and comprehensible. And there is the rub.

This volume both overviews the area of LPE and demonstrates the tension caused by utility and rigor constantly pulling at each other. My introduction (Chapter One) provides some background on the legislative environment and outlines the organizational framework for this volume.

Acknowledgments

A number of thanks are due. This volume would not have happened without Gary Henry's support and encouragement. I also owe personal thanks to two people on the Joint Legislative Audit and Review Commission (JLARC) staff, my LPE agency. Philip A. Leone, JLARC's staff director, supported this effort throughout. John Long, JLARC's publications editor, provided invaluable editorial and computer support.

I also thank the authors. They have been unusually patient with me as an editor. While some in the various legislatures might appreciate their efforts on this project, I expect that for most of the authors, this was a labor of professional satisfaction.

R. Kirk Jonas
Editor

R. KIRK JONAS is deputy director of the Joint Legislative Audit and Review Commission of the Virginia General Assembly and an adjunct professor in the University of Richmond Department of Political Science.

Evaluation capabilities of the nation's state legislatures provide a unique resource to the overall evaluation community.

Against the Whim: State Legislatures' Use of Program Evaluation

R. Kirk Jonas

Legislative program evaluation (LPE) agencies have come into their own during the past two decades. Evaluation capabilities of state legislatures are relatively new, given the ancient (by American standards) origins of some legislatures. Most legislative evaluation agencies grew indirectly out of the overall modernization initiatives of legislatures during the 1970s. John Burns's *The Sometimes Governments* (1971) presented many of the nation's legislatures as ineffective clubs, a weak link in the federal system. This critical book struck many within the nation's legislatures as true and was a galvanizing influence on reformers in many states. The effect of this realization was that legislators saw the need to rely less on information generated by executive branch agencies and more on resources under their direct control.

Moreover, as the information capabilities and expectations of members and citizens alike have increased, there has been a discernible rationalization of the legislative process. Accountability has become increasingly important, and the whims of individual politicians often have had to take a back seat to the rational justification of public policies. Responding to the unique demands of this environment, LPE organizations have emerged, developing procedures, methods, and vocabularies that promise to add value to the overall field of evaluation.

During the 1970s and 1980s, legislatures became more empowered institutions. They created committee staffs, particularly in the finance areas. Member services and facilities were enhanced. Legislators' salaries increased. Women

The views expressed in this chapter are the author's and should not be construed as representing those of the Virginia Joint Legislative Audit and Review Commission.

and minorities achieved substantial inclusion. Legislatures established or strengthened financial audit capabilities. And they created program evaluation units. The legislatures of the 1990s are a far cry from the "sometime governments" of the 1960s, which had difficulty comprehending, much less evaluating, executive branch initiatives and programs.

One of the signature steps in the evolution of the modern legislature was the development of program evaluation capabilities. With this step, legislatures added the structural focus of the legislative oversight function to their traditional roles, such as lawmaking, appropriation of funds, and constituent services. Through the oversight function, legislatures attended to the business of ensuring that legislative intent was met and that the programs they established or funded were operating efficiently, effectively, and economically. The oversight function was strengthened through either the establishment of independent program evaluation units or the assignment of the performance auditing function to existing financial auditing units. Legislatures have always exercised some degree of oversight over the executive branch. For example, committees have hearings. Members listen to constituents and interest groups, and employees talk about programs and agencies, both good and bad. If a program or agency is known or even perceived to be weak, it can have its statute changed or its budget cut. Information and analysis are provided to the legislature at an organizational, or actionable, level. LPE units have empowered legislatures to demand more refined responses to their interests and concerns.

Today a strong program evaluation capability exists in a majority of state legislatures, where virtually none existed thirty years ago. At least forty states have a program evaluation capability. In some states the legislative evaluation capability grew out of existing financial auditing organizations and remains there as a section or function (Wisler, 1996). In other states the evaluation capability was created independent of the audit function. With the growth of this capability, an interesting niche of the program evaluation community has emerged. Although LPE has strong roots in the overall evaluation community, it has unique characteristics and a strong utilization focus that add value to the larger field.

LPE continues to evolve. On the horizon are changes that promise to challenge LPE organizations in a variety of ways. As devolution pushes more national programs down to the states and localities, LPE units will likely play a lead role in evaluating the diverse programs that emerge. In addition, as the structure of governments is complicated by privatization and outsourcing initiatives, LPE units will find themselves contracting for and overseeing complex private sector evaluation contracts, often in the information technology area. These changes will likely challenge the field in a positive, adaptive way. The emergence of term limits will likely pose a challenge of a different type. Eighteen states now have legislative term limitations (Bell, 1998), and it remains to be seen whether this phenomenon will strengthen or weaken oversight generally and LPE specifically.

I believe the field of LPE is sufficiently mature to shoulder the burden of such changing conditions and expanded roles. In many states it has moved beyond the narrower financial auditing roots of its origin and adds discernible value to the overall field of program evaluation in a number of ways—for example:

- Its focus on utilization affects both the language and techniques of evaluation, often the result of performing studies under legislative mandate.
- The systematic development of databases has provided raw information on government programs, activities, and accomplishments.
- Far-reaching study findings have resulted from virtually unlimited access to state-level databases that contain information from individual files, such as criminal records or tax records.
- Adaptive research methods have resulted from study mandates that impose time frames and require a combination of evaluative, operational, and policy perspectives.

Program evaluators in the context of the legislative arena have developed utilization-focused approaches that are a combination of science, craft, and art. The science consists of the academic foundations of good research. The craft is the accumulated expertise that legislative evaluators accrue with experience. And the art is the combination of individual skills and intuition that each researcher develops as he or she practices the trade.

The Context: Utilization-Obsessed Evaluation

LPE is characterized by an obsession with utilization. Unlike evaluations that have knowledge development as their primary purpose, there is little pure science in LPE. Utilization is not accidental, however. Good evaluation offices improve the prospects for utilization through responsiveness, relevance, language, and quality.

The purposes of LPE begin and end with the need for useful knowledge. As Don Bezruki, Janice Mueller, and Karen McKim state in Chapter Two, one of the defining characteristics of LPE is "its emphasis on utilization. State legislatures have created staff agencies, or designated units within existing agencies, to perform program evaluations for the express purpose of using evaluation results in the conduct of legislative business." This chapter examines the development and utilization of three evaluations conducted by the Wisconsin Legislative Audit Bureau. The authors use the three evaluation reports that the bureau prepared to illustrate types of utilization resulting from legislatively mandated evaluations. In each case, "report utilization served to inform and, in some cases, structure legislative decision making." The authors argue that the "the extent to which the audit bureau's work is meaningful...depends on whether the information it develops provides any value to the legislature." Further, an analysis of the examples presented and resulting study outcomes provides perspective on how evaluation design and implementation can affect utilization and, conversely, how the expectation of utilization can affect evaluation design.

Another facet of legislative utilization of program evaluation can be seen on a more conceptual level. A legislature may use evaluations to assess the effectiveness of new governance approaches. For example, privatization of governmental functions has been an ongoing initiative of reformers seeking to reduce the base costs of government. Privatization initiatives are often promoted not only as cost-saving measures but also as a means of limiting the size and scope of government. In Chapter Three Robert C. Thomas, Kathy Gookin, Beth Keating, and Valerie Whitener discuss means of ensuring that "the public sector captures some of the savings" promised by privatization. The evaluation of privatized functions is clearly an area where LPE can expect to be involved. The authors note that "support for privatization is increasing among state governments" and "interest in cost savings is a major driver in this trend." The authors, who participated in studies evaluating the cost savings potential from privatization, demonstrate that "arriving at a best estimate of actual costs, and the costs that can be avoided with privatization, is a difficult task, and errors are always possible." They provide eight general guidelines for minimizing privatization risks, including the establishment of performance monitoring and oversight.

Conditions and Methods of LPE That Add Value to the Field

LPE's focus on utilization creates some unique conditions, methods, approaches, and products that add overall value to the field of program evaluation. Evaluators can look to LPE for a variety of such qualities:

- Extraordinary access to information, including the presentation (in aggregate form) of protected records
- The application of "out-of-the-box" approaches to evaluation problems
- The use of convergent approaches to strengthen findings in complex study areas
- Utilization of new technologies for creation of databases

Access to Information. LPE organizations enjoy virtually unlimited access to information. This is particularly true for state and local programs, most often the subject of LPE inquiry. The legislative evaluator has degrees of lateral and vertical access that open study possibilities that are more often envied than emulated. In Chapter Four I discuss the impact that such access has had on a variety of studies by the Joint Legislative Audit and Review Commission (JLARC) of the Virginia General Assembly. Access to individual client files, tax records, agency records, and employees themselves have enabled JLARC to assess areas that are usually beyond the reach of academic or media inquiry. In addition, the long-term existence of an agency such as JLARC allows for longitudinal and comparative studies that cannot be performed on a contractual basis. Current performance reviews of state agencies, for example, can include comparisons of employee morale with similar assessments done in the past or at other agencies.

The value that this aspect of LPE adds to the field is not so much unique as it is concentrated. If good records management and protection is provided, the legislative evaluator can expect (or require) access to everything from tax records to patient files. Reports based on such protected data can provide evaluators with insights on programs that are often unavailable from other sources.

"Out-of-the-Box" Methodological Approaches. A variety of innovative methodological applications are also being adapted, used, and advanced by LPE organizations. In Chapter Five Patrick W. McIntire and Ann S. Glaze of Oregon's Legislative Fiscal Office describe the efforts of that office to address the dual problems of system complexity and data constraints. The authors discuss the development of a systems model of state and local organizations using ithink® software. This approach enabled them "to evaluate comprehensive effects of current and potential policy and management decisions on stated and assumed goals."

As the authors note, legislation "is often comprehensive so that several aspects of one or more agencies or issues are concurrently affected. Common evaluation techniques do not easily enable assessments of interactive and concurrent effects of these complex mandates." Systems modeling, or computer simulation, was used in the Oregon Legislative Fiscal Office's program evaluation of the Oregon Commission on Children and Families (OCCF). An example of the kind of devolution that is occurring at the state or substate level, the OCCF is "an organization of county commissions and a central state agency intended to provide preventive, locally integrated services for children and families." Evaluators will be interested to note that the outcome performance measures for the program were linked to the well-known Oregon Benchmarks, which have received national attention from a variety of sources, including Vice President Gore's National Performance Review.

The results of the modeling exercise are instructive. McIntire and Glaze note that lack of data did limit their ability to validate the model fully, an outcome not unexpected in public policy research. This lack of data, and the expectation that appropriate data may never exist, lead the authors to conclude that "staff need to research and implement accurate qualitative methodologies to provide appropriate information, especially regarding management effectiveness, to continue evaluation programs, including modeling exercises." Nonetheless, the modeling exercise was valuable and contributed to a better understanding of the organization and processes of the OCCF. In particular, the authors doubted that analysts would have discovered "the overall system behavior" through techniques more familiar to the legislature. As other states experience devolved programs, they may find the application of similar modeling approaches to be valuable means of understanding the complex new organizations they have created.

Convergence Approaches. One of the realities of LPE is that topics mandated for study are not always good fits with a single methodological approach.

The legislature rarely frames study mandates with research feasibility in mind. Complex problems arise and legislative evaluators are asked to analyze these problems. In Chapter Six Desmond Saunders-Newton, Gregory J. Rest, and Wayne M. Turnage discuss the use of multiple research methods to address the question of whether the siting of solid waste facilities targeted minority communities. They emphasize the "importance of designing policy studies and program evaluations in a fashion that allows for using the results from disparate techniques such that they 'converge' on similar policy solutions. This approach allows for the generation of preponderant evidence in support of a given social outcome or policy recommendation."

Utilization of New Technologies. A broader environmental challenge to the evaluation community in general is how to apply emerging technologies to LPE. Florida's Office of Program Policy Analysis and Government Accountability (OPPAGA) has been designing an evaluation report that may presage similar initiatives elsewhere. Gena C. Wade reports in Chapter Seven on the Florida Government Accountability Report (FGAR), which uses delivery methods and content that vary from traditional evaluation reports. Located on the World Wide Web, the FGAR contains "descriptive information and summaries of the status of evaluation on individual state programs, but it differs dramatically from past OPPAGA products in that it will contain a letter rating on the quality of state programs' accountability systems." Information currency will increase dramatically, as will the accessibility of data, not only to the evaluation community but to the public as a whole. As performance measurement systems are tried nationwide, the FGAR system may provide a glimpse of an evaluation community oriented more to emerging electronic technologies than traditional book-type reports.

From Knowledge to Language

One of the key factors defining LPE is the diversity of its clients or users—the legislators themselves. No longer the "clubs" of earlier times, legislatures are increasingly demographically representative of our diverse nation. The legislative arena is a kind of policy development cauldron. The most representative of our political institutions, legislatures are a rich mix of creative and reactionary forces, innovations and traditions, ambition and statesmanship. Legislatures are a paradigm of paradoxes. Because of the special demands of this environment, there are unique communication demands on LPE agencies.

Nancy C. Zajano and Shannon S. Lochtefeld focus in Chapter Eight on the language required to communicate useful knowledge to legislators. They describe the nature of knowledge generated for special legislative demands and the language that has evolved to communicate that knowledge. Zajano and Lochtefeld discuss the need for evaluators to provide accessible evaluation findings in an environment that leaves "almost no time for thoughtful reflection or reading." They note that the legislature is "predominantly an oral culture." Although the field as a whole may not want (or need) to go to the extremes used by legislative program evaluators to make their work useful to legislators, most competent evaluators become interested in the implementation of their findings and recommendations. (Indeed, the opportunity for meaningful implementation is one of the rewarding facets of a career in LPE.) The first step toward implementation is encouraging familiarity with the research, that is, making sure the client knows what the evaluator has learned. Perhaps no other branch of evaluation has devoted as much energy to facilitating utilization as has LPE. Language, then, takes on an importance in LPE that is both necessary and instructive.

Future Directions in LPE

Constructive challenges for LPE in the states will originate from both within and outside the legislative environment and from within the field itself. Devolution of federal programs, applications of emerging technologies, and term limits all signal substantial challenges to legislative program evaluators.

The balance of responsibilities among the various levels of government within the federal system is perennially shifting. In the 1930s the forces of economic depression, political unrest, and shifting political influence began a process of centralizing functions previously operated at the state and local levels, if at all. For example, urban widows and orphans programs, state welfare systems, and various fragmented safety nets were unified under the Social Security Act of 1935. After various manifestations of "new federalism," such as the revenue-sharing programs of the 1970s, a pattern commonly referred to as devolution has emerged. The most dramatic example of this trend is the replacement of the Aid for Families with Dependent Children (AFDC) program with the Temporary Assistance to Needy Families (TANF) programs. While AFDC was a relatively structured and consistent program, TANF initiatives are exceptionally diverse. States have tremendous latitude in these programs, and accountability will necessarily reside primarily at the state level. Evaluations of such devolved programs will likely fall to state LPE organizations, a formidable challenge. Another challenge will be institutional in nature. Almost half of current LPE agencies will be influenced, in ways difficult to predict, by term limits.

Term Limits. Complicating the future of LPE (and legislative institutions generally) is the term limit movement. Eighteen states now operate under some type of legislative term limitation. In term limit states, house members are limited to tenures between six and twelve years (most are eight-year limits), and senate members are limited to between eight and twelve years (again, most are eight-year limits). Rakesh Mohan and Mary Stutzman suggest in Chapter Nine that oversight is one of the subtler legislative functions. Consequently there is a concern in the LPE community that the function will not be fully understood or appreciated by short-term legislators.

Successful oversight depends on members with memory, as one of the principal functions of oversight is to determine the extent of compliance with legislative intent. In the past, senior legislators reviewing a program often had been directly involved in the creation or reformulation of that program. Continuity of service (at least among more senior members) was one of the advantages most legislatures enjoyed over the executive branch. This advantage may be lost in states that have adopted legislative term limits.

Conclusion

LPE is a dynamic area within the larger field of program evaluation. It is utilization focused because its customer—the legislature—demands useful knowledge "in plain English." At the same time, probable utilization raises the stakes for evaluators. Studies that are likely to be used must be thoughtfully designed and rigorously executed. Responding to these challenges, legislative program evaluators have produced work that adds value to the processes, methods, and language of the overall field.

Program evaluation in state legislatures is enjoying a period of appreciation and success. It has helped legislatures achieve a higher level of information parity with governors and executive agencies. Success brings with it different challenges, however. Evaluators must necessarily work between the boundaries of evaluation and policy analysis. This creates methodological and process challenges. In addition, because LPE demands useful knowledge, programs and program changes based on past evaluations will themselves require scrutiny. All in all, the legislative area of program evaluation promises not to be dull for years to come.

Much fine work is being done by LPE agencies that are not represented or discussed in this volume. Many of these organizations have extensive and useful web sites, often including full reports in downloadable formats, that can be useful resources to researchers seeking information on state programs and policies. Links to these sites can be gained through the National Conference of State Legislatures (NCSL) web site: http://www.ncsl.org. In addition, most legislative evaluation units participate in the National LPE Section of NCSL. The NLPES web site currently contains links to legislative evaluation agencies in twenty-two states. The NLPES site is: http://www.oppaga.state.fl.us/NLPES. Finally, those seeking further information are invited to contact me, KJonas@leg.state.va.us.

References

Bell, D. "Time's Up!" *State Legislatures,* 1998, Jul.-Aug., pp. 24–29.
Burns, J. *The Sometimes Governments.* New York: Bantam Books, 1971.
Wisler, C. (ed.). *Evaluation and Auditing: Prospects for Convergence.* New Directions for Evaluation, no. 71. San Francisco: Jossey-Bass, 1996.

R. KIRK JONAS is deputy director of the Virginia Joint Legislative Audit and Review Commission of the Virginia General Assembly and an adjunct professor in the University of Richmond Department of Political Science.

The emphasis on utilization, a primary characteristic of legislative
program evaluation, can influence evaluation design.

Legislative Utilization of Evaluations

Don Bezruki, Janice Mueller, Karen McKim

Utilization of evaluation results has long been a focus of discussion by evaluation theorists and practitioners alike. Although there has been extensive research on how to enhance utilization, there are also concerns that efforts to increase utilization could impair evaluator independence and lead to questions about the credibility or accuracy of evaluation findings. Most recently, Shulha and Cousins (1997) have provided an overview of recent discussions of utilization and identified emerging developments.

Utilization of evaluations performed by staff agencies of state legislatures has many forms. Fundamentally such program evaluation supports legislative oversight of the executive branch by providing information about the implementation and results of executive branch programs. Legislatures use this information in a variety of ways—passing laws that create, modify, or eliminate programs; making budget decisions; and jawboning executive branch officials to make management or programmatic changes. In the legislative environment, utilization extends considerably beyond direct implementation of formal recommendations included in evaluation reports.

In Wisconsin the legislature has demonstrated sustained interest in both the "fire alarm" and "police patrol" oversight strategies that Wohlstetter (1990) identified. Although many requests for evaluations are made in response to alarms or reports in the media of troubles with a particular program, requests for evaluations are also frequently included in enabling legislation as a program is created or significantly modified. Increasingly legislatures are asking evaluation agencies to go beyond evaluating the fiscal accountability of executive branch agencies or the efficiency of programs, to ask about programmatic accountability. Legislatures are using evaluations of program outcomes to make decisions about program design and funding. Although the types of evaluations conducted continue to evolve and increase in number, a constant is their focus on utilization.

As a result of the differing nature of the requests and the information desired by the legislature, the Wisconsin Legislative Audit Bureau conducts various types of evaluations, from multiyear experimental design studies of program outcomes, to assessments of management and program implementation in relation to legislative intent, to investigations of alleged wrongdoing by executive branch officials. For example, an evaluation of whether pregnancy prevention programs succeed in actually reducing pregnancy rates among participants served as the basis for legislative actions to modify the programs. An evaluation of whether programs for youth at risk of dropping out of school succeeded in lowering dropout rates and improving school achievement resulted in significant redirection of the program by the legislature.

In some cases, changes are made to program design in order to effect changes in program outcomes, but program outcomes can also be affected through changes to organizational operations. Here we look at three examples of how public officials in Wisconsin used legislative program evaluations to change the way in which agencies operated in order to improve program outcomes or meet other legislative goals. The first describes how legislators used evaluation results to pass legislation designed to increase the accountability of a state agency and reassure public confidence. The second describes how legislators used the results of an evaluation to pass legislation designed to improve state regulatory oversight of a private industry, in this case nursing homes. The third describes how state and local officials used evaluation results to restructure a local antipoverty agency and pressure its management to implement administrative changes. In each case the evaluations provided public officials with objective and reliable information about the nature of a program and any problems, and provided practical recommendations and options for action. Analysis of these examples and their outcomes may provide some perspective on how evaluation design and implementation can affect utilization and, conversely, how expectations of utilization can affect evaluation design.

Evaluation of the State of Wisconsin Investment Board

The evaluation of the State of Wisconsin Investment Board demonstrates how legislators used evaluation results to restore confidence in the board by making statutory changes to improve accountability and ensure better oversight of investment decisions. Here is the summary of the evaluation:

BASIS OF REQUEST OF EVALUATION
- Loss of $95 million in highly speculative investments
- Concern over potential loss of confidence in the investment board

EVALUATION FINDINGS
- The board had insufficient controls to guide the use of speculative investments.

- Staff were uninformed of details of derivative investments.
- Oversight of investment decisions was inadequate.

LEGISLATIVE UTILIZATION

- Legislation was enacted that changed board composition and structure, created new staff positions to oversee investment decisions, and improved legislative oversight of the board.

Basis of Request for Evaluation. The State of Wisconsin Investment Board is responsible for investing and managing the assets of the pension system for state and most local government employees and teachers and the cash balances of the state and most local units of government. Late one Friday afternoon, the investment board issued a short press release announcing that the investment fund had incurred a $95 million loss as a result of investments in derivatives. These financial instruments, whose value depends on or is "derived" from the value of one or more underlying assets or indexes of asset values, can be highly speculative. Derivatives were involved in large losses of public funds in Orange County, California, and in several large private sector companies during 1994.

Within days of the disclosure, seven legislators requested an audit of various aspects of the investment board. Their concerns included the adequacy of investment policies; the board's degree of exposure to risky investments; potential loss of investor confidence in the board, which could result in participants' withdrawing from the board's funds; and the effect on bond ratings.

Evaluation Findings. The evaluation concluded that in an attempt to achieve higher returns, the investment board had turned increasingly to less traditional investments, including investing in international markets, and to riskier investments such as derivative instruments, but without sufficient controls to guide their use. This degree of risk taking was clearly inappropriate for the state investment fund, which had a conservative investment policy designed to ensure liquidity of assets.

The report provided a detailed chronology of events leading to the public disclosure of the derivative loss. Of the $95 million loss, $35 million was attributable to one swap agreement involving Mexican interest rates. Although investment board staff contended that they were misled by the dealer in the swap agreement, the evaluation found that board staff lacked understanding of the detailed terms of the derivative.

Effective management oversight mechanisms might have prompted investment staff to perform necessary and thorough analyses of the initial investments, identified the magnitude of the problem derivatives earlier, and prevented the investment director's unilateral and costly action to restructure the Mexican swap. However, the evaluation concluded that management failed to detect problems because of the board's decentralized organizational structure, weak operating controls, and inadequate management oversight mechanisms. Although some delegation is essential in the fast-paced investment arena, the evaluation concluded that within the investment board, the principle of delegated authority was carried to an extreme.

To avoid problems in the future, the evaluation recommended the board change its organizational culture and increase controls over investment strategy and reporting. The evaluation report included a number of recommendations to improve investment guidelines, reporting, and monitoring, so that the investment board's staff and members of its board of trustees could better manage its investments. The report also suggested options for organizational improvements similar to those used in other states, such as employing a chief investment officer or internal auditor to increase oversight of investment decision making.

Legislative Utilization. Legislative and public responses to the evaluation's disclosures were immediate. On the day the evaluation was released, the senate cochair of the Joint Legislative Audit Committee said, in a press release on July 10, 1995, "State Investment Board officials were operating in the dark when they entered into risky derivatives. . . . This could have been a financial doomsday." The *Milwaukee Journal Sentinel* (1997) editorialized, "Notably and with good reason, the state audit urges more oversight, noting specifically that the board's senior management failed to exercise proper control over lower-level staffers who invested in the complicated derivatives."

The Joint Legislative Audit Committee held two public hearings on the report, and companion bills were introduced in the assembly and the senate to accelerate legislative deliberations. Within three months of their introduction, both bills passed their respective houses with no dissenting votes, and the final bill was signed by the governor.

On the day after the bill passed the Wisconsin Assembly, the assembly cochair of the Audit Committee said, in a press release on January 26, 1996, "The State Assembly took the appropriate steps to bring closure to the problems associated with the $95 million loss in the State Investment Fund. We have put in place the needed reforms to prevent future losses due to speculative and inappropriate investments."

The legislation made significant changes to improve oversight of the board, change the composition and structure of the board of trustees, restrict the use of derivative investments, and expand the authority of the Legislative Audit Bureau to audit the board. Based directly on the evaluation's recommendations, the new legislation took the following actions:

• Expanded the board of trustees to include a representative of the local governments that invest in the fund
• Required the board to keep full minutes of its proceedings
• Created new positions, including a chief investment officer and an internal auditor, to improve oversight of investment decisions and provide improved information to the board concerning staff compliance with board investment policies
• Restricted the use of certain types of investments, including prohibiting the purchase or acquisition of derivative instruments except in accordance with rules promulgated by the board
• Statutorily defined a derivative instrument

- Required the board to report annually to the legislature on investment goals and long-term strategies and the types of investments it held, including information on their market values and degree of risk; and to report changes in investment policies and guidelines as they are implemented
- Required the Legislative Audit Bureau to conduct annual financial audits that would include the board's internal control structure, as well as biennial performance audits of the board's policies and management practices

Since the report's release, both a chief investment officer and internal auditor have been hired; reports on investment holdings and the board's activities have been produced and reviewed carefully by the legislature's Joint Legislative Audit Committee; and the first biennial performance audit conducted by the Legislative Audit Bureau under the provisions of the legislation was scheduled to begin in January 1999. There has been no recurrence of derivative losses.

Evaluation of Nursing Home Regulation

The evaluation of nursing home regulation demonstrates how legislators used evaluation results to determine the effectiveness of state regulatory oversight and to identify weaknesses in oversight statutes. Here is the summary:

BASIS OF REQUEST FOR EVALUATION
- Reports of nurse aide misconduct were investigated only after lengthy delay.
- Regulatory officials were not adequately enforcing nursing home regulations.

EVALUATION FINDINGS
- There were a relatively small number of problem homes.
- Regulatory officials imposed light, delayed penalties for repeat violations.
- Ombudsman staffing was inadequate.

LEGISLATIVE UTILIZATION
- Legislation was passed to increase penalties for problem homes, increase ombudsmen staffing, increase minimum staff in homes, and improve consumer protection methods.

Basis of Request for Evaluation. A March 1997 series of articles in the *Milwaukee Journal Sentinel* (Zahn and Umhoefer, 1997), the state's largest newspaper, described ineffective regulatory action by the state Department of Health and Family Services, which has responsibility for enforcing both state and federal nursing home standards. The newspaper reported that the department was taking eight months to resolve some cases of reported misconduct by state-certified nurse aides and was imposing relatively light and significantly delayed penalties for serious and repeat violations of nursing homes' quality-of-care regulations.

Legislators requested an evaluation to investigate the problems reported by the newspaper, as well as other legislative concerns, including the adequacy of state-imposed minimum nursing home staffing requirements and of the state-operated nursing home ombudsman program. Legislation to strengthen penalties for violations of state nursing home regulations was introduced with the intent that action would not be scheduled until completion of the evaluation.

Evaluation Findings. Due to the breadth of the issues identified in the request, the evaluation was divided into two parts: the first evaluated the handling of complaints of certified nurse aides' misconduct (theft, abuse, or neglect), and the second evaluated the enforcement of other nursing home regulations.

Delay in resolution of misconduct complaints was more serious than the newspaper had reported. The evaluation found that although federal regulations require "timely and swift" response to complaints and state regulations require investigations to be completed within sixty days, the average time between a complaint's filing and its resolution was eleven months for all cases resolved during the program's six-year history. Among a sample of seventy cases, no investigations had been initiated until eight months after the complaint was received, and resolution had taken as long as thirty-six months.

The delays in nurse aide misconduct investigation were caused by administrative shortcomings: the department had designed an inefficient complaint-resolution process, failed to document investigative procedures properly, and failed to exercise adequate management oversight. Management oversight was so limited that the department could not identify or count all pending cases; evaluators had to do this. Most program staff were unaware of the time limits governing their tasks. Seven detailed recommendations were addressed to the department and covered nearly all stages of the complaint-resolution process.

The administrative shortcomings in the regulation of nursing homes were not as extensive as critics had feared. For example, the department promptly investigated complaints of matters other than nurse aide misconduct. However, the evaluation found other problems, many of them caused by weak or outdated statutes and regulations and therefore amenable to legislative action. For example, certain state regulations—particularly staffing regulations—were being ignored because they were outdated. Statutes governing the imposition of forfeitures for repeat violations were written so that the department could adopt a narrow definition of "repeat violation" that would allow it to reduce or even omit forfeitures for even serious and repeated violations. The report identified statutory amendments that could increase the consistency with which the stricter penalties were imposed.

Finally, the evaluation found that the nursing home ombudsman program, which employs advocates for long-term-care residents who serve as informal "eyes and ears" for the department's inspectors, was staffed at a level half that of the median among other states, and one-third of that recommended by the federal Institute of Medicine.

Legislative Utilization. Within four months of the release of the evaluation, the department used the report's conclusions and recommendations to develop methods for improving investigation and resolution of nurse aide misconduct allegations, and the legislature used the report to strengthen statutes governing regulation of nursing homes.

The department implemented recommendations to strengthen and expedite investigations by improving written guidelines for the misconduct complaint-resolution process, adopting additional written guidance and improving training for the misconduct investigators, allowing for the entry of admission of guilt by accused nurse aides, improving management oversight of the program, and reassigning some staff. As a result of these changes, the number of misconduct complaints awaiting investigation has been reduced so that they can be resolved within the sixty-day limit.

The evaluation also provided useful focus to the public policy debate regarding penalties for violations of nursing home regulations by defining and quantifying the concept of "problem homes." Advocates for stronger penalties were basing their arguments on the incidence of repeat violations, while the nursing home industry argued that repeat violations could happen at random regardless of a nursing home's efforts to improve.

The evaluation developed the concept of an "unresponsive home," defined as one that in each of three consecutive inspections had more than two serious violations or was in the worst 10 percent of all homes when ranked by number of violations. This analysis showed that the large majority of nursing homes respond effectively to enforcement activities but that a relatively small number of unresponsive problem homes did in fact exist. This information demonstrated that strict penalties levied against such homes would affect only a few nursing homes, not the entire industry. The focus on the existence of a few nursing homes with truly indefensible records enabled legislators to draft bills that would affect the most serious problems, which made opposition to legislative action more difficult and increased bipartisan support.

Upon the release of the report, evaluators met with the assembly sponsor of the pending forfeitures bill and the committee chairperson to discuss possible amendments to reflect the recommendations. Evaluators testified before the legislative committee, which eventually passed the forfeiture bill on a six-to-three vote.

A separate bill was introduced to increase minimum staffing requirements for nursing homes, clarify distribution requirements for consumer information reports, and add positions to the state's long-term-care ombudsmen agency. This bill passed a different committee unanimously. Shortly after both bills were referred to the legislature's finance committee, the legislative session ended without additional action on either bill. However, a special session of the legislature was subsequently convened, and provisions of the two bills were incorporated into an omnibus budget bill, which passed the legislature and was signed by the governor.

Evaluation of the Social Development Commission

The evaluation of the Social Development Commission (SDC), the largest antipoverty agency in Milwaukee County (Wisconsin's most populous county), demonstrates how state and local policymakers used evaluation results to discern the causes of programmatic shortcomings and as a basis for policy decisions about an agency's mission and governance structure. Here is the summary:

BASIS OF REQUEST FOR EVALUATION
- Problems with service delivery to the public.
- Financial management problems, including resignations of the treasurer and finance officer.
- Lack of confidence by external funding agencies.

EVALUATION FINDINGS
- Financial and program management problems were systemic.
- Management problems hampered service delivery.
- Governance problems inhibited leadership and oversight.

LEGISLATIVE UTILIZATION
- The agency was pressured by state and local elected officials to implement internal restructuring and numerous management changes.
- County and city ordinances were rewritten to reform governance structure.

Basis for Request of Evaluation. Over a six-month period, media in the Milwaukee area reported a series of stories about apparent financial and management problems at the Social Development Commission. The SDC's $26 million annual budget, which provided over seventy programs ranging from Head Start to numerous social services and jobs programs, was funded by grants and unrestricted funds from the federal, state, county, and city governments, as well as from United Way, the Milwaukee School Board, and others. SDC was governed by a twenty-four-member board and employed 450 staff. The media articles described a failed multimillion-dollar construction project, the resignations of the agency's treasurer and its chief financial officer amid rumors that they had been prevented from adequately carrying out their fiduciary responsibilities, allegations that the chair of the agency's governing board had used the agency credit card for personal purchases, assertions by the executive director of mysterious break-ins at agency offices and the theft of financial records, and reports of poor service delivery.

The legislature's assembly majority leader and others requested the audit, indicating the need to restore accountability to the agency. Several days after the Joint Legislative Audit Committee directed that an evaluation be undertaken, the chair of the Milwaukee County Board of Supervisors directed the Milwaukee County Department of Audit to undertake a similar audit of SDC. The two audit agencies agreed to coordinate their work and subsequently issued a joint report.

Evaluation Findings. The report contained forty specific recommendations, including steps for improving governance and management of the agency and its programs. In addition, the report provided a number of options for the legislature and local authorities to consider in addressing the larger questions of restructuring agency governance.

After confirming the existence and extent of the management problems that had been alleged, the evaluation identified numerous other problems and demonstrated how the significant patterns of inadequate management had both undermined administrative functions and contributed to problems with service delivery and programs. It concluded that existing administrative policies and procedures, such as fiscal controls, purchasing guidelines, personnel procedures, and others, were routinely overridden by management and that no systems existed to monitor agency performance or compel staff compliance with procedures.

The report demonstrated that the management problems had continued because the agency's board had failed to perform its leadership and oversight roles. The evaluation found that the governing board's committees, especially the finance committee, had weak and ill-defined charges; both the ill-fated food service construction project and the agency's annual budget had been approved without review or discussion by the finance committee. Similarly, committee officers had unclear responsibilities and authority, and the local governments and community organizations that appointed board members were not exercising adequate oversight of their appointees. During the evaluation, the executive director of the agency, the chair of the agency's governing board, and the board's legal counsel all resigned under pressure.

Legislative Utilization. State and local officials used the evaluation to compel management changes at the agency and as a basis for decisions to restructure the agency's governance. Before the report was issued, there was considerable public debate within the community and among state officials about the veracity of many of the allegations about SDC and the extent to which problems existed. Because of the independence and objectivity of the two audit agencies, the report was accepted as the most authoritative and accurate account of the current condition of SDC and the causes of the problems. After the report was issued, the evaluators conducted numerous private briefings of state and local elected officials and testified at a public hearing held jointly by the state Joint Legislative Audit Committee and a review committee established by the chairperson of the County Board's Finance and Audit Committee.

The evaluation enabled interested parties to focus on improving both the agency and service delivery. For example, as a result of the report's findings, state and local officials exerted immediate pressure on SDC to implement the report's twenty-four recommendations for management changes. The heads of the state Department of Corrections and Department of Health and Family Services served notice that they were suspending some existing grants and would not renew others totaling several hundred thousand dollars without documentation of SDC's compliance with recommendations. Similarly, over $500,000 in unrestricted funding to the agency was withheld by the City of Milwaukee, Milwaukee County, and other local funding organizations pending significant improvements in agency management. The County Board's

Finance and Audit Committee directed the county audit department to monitor SDC's implementation of each of the twenty-four recommendations and report regularly on the agency's progress.

The evaluation also served as a basis for discussion and for decisions among state and local elected officials to address governance problems. Although the report contained sixteen recommendations to improve the governing board's structure and operations, it also suggested that the board did not have the institutional capacity to address its problems alone and could require outside assistance. Upon release of the evaluation, the speaker of the state assembly appointed a task force of fifteen local community leaders to develop recommendations on changing the mission and nature of the agency.

Although SDC was originally created by city and county ordinance, the authority for local officials to do so was granted by state statute, and the evaluation's findings prompted discussions in the state legislature about making statutory changes that would have eliminated the agency. To continue local control in the light of the potential state legislative action, the chair of the Milwaukee County Board of Supervisors and the president of the City of Milwaukee Common Council reviewed the conclusions of the speaker's task force and developed a proposal similar to one of the options presented in the evaluation: maintaining SDC as a public agency but reducing the size of the board, changing board member appointment methods, and strengthening board procedures. Subsequently the city and the county modified their local ordinances to abolish the existing board and establish a transitional board with full governing authority. Based on the evaluation's recommendations and analyses, the transitional board developed bylaws and specific operating procedures so the new board committees and officers could carry out their leadership and oversight responsibilities. In addition, the transitional board followed the audit's suggestions for decreasing the size of the permanent board to make board deliberations more manageable and for modifying the appointment process to allow greater accountability.

Within two years of the evaluation report's release, all management recommendations had been implemented, recommendations for changes in the bylaws and operating procedures of the governing board had been made, local ordinances had been amended to change the governance structure of the agency, and a new permanent board was in place.

Conclusion

A defining characteristic of legislative program evaluation is its emphasis on utilization. State legislatures have created staff agencies or designated units within existing agencies to perform program evaluations for the express purpose of using evaluation results in the conduct of legislative business. The three evaluations described were used extensively by legislators and other decision makers to change programs, policy, and management. In one of the cases, legislative action on a previously introduced bill was postponed until the evaluation was completed and the results and recommendations were available.

The expectation of use by the legislature and others influences evaluation design. An evaluation design that fails to anticipate use, such as failing to evaluate questions of legislative concern or to provide results within the legislative calendar, will undermine the utilization of the evaluation results. For example, an evaluation that concludes that a job placement program is successful in placing clients in jobs but does not answer legislative questions about availability of the program throughout the state will be of limited use to legislators.

Legislative evaluations must be designed so that final reports accurately and objectively inform the legislature and other readers of the actual condition of the program or activity being evaluated. Prior to the release of an evaluation, legislators' and other decision makers' knowledge of a program or issue is often shaped by information that may be biased, speculative, incomplete, or anecdotal. To be credible and useful to the legislature, an evaluation must apply defensible research techniques to describe convincingly a program's condition—either the outcomes of the program or the status of program implementation—in a way that recognizes and addresses the numerous preexisting beliefs and assumptions about the program and creates a shared understanding for discussion to proceed.

In most states, legislative evaluations are also expected to offer practical options for action. A common question legislators pose at briefings on evaluations is, "What does the report expect the legislature to do?" Although legislators guard their prerogative to accept or reject recommendations, the issue of action is of primary importance.

This responsibility to provide options for action requires that the evaluation design allow the evaluation to go beyond describing a program's condition to identifying the causes that led to the condition, especially if results deviate from legislative expectations. Identification of these causes, such as improper implementation, poor management, inadequate program design, or insufficient resources, is critical for the development of practical, effective recommendations. For example, the evaluation of the SDC provided practical options for structuring the agency's governance while retaining local control. Similarly, the evaluation of the investment board contained recommendations designed to improve oversight of, and confidence in, the board while leaving the board adequate flexibility to make investment decisions. Practical recommendations or options are essential to legislators, who define their roles as taking action to address problems or needs. Evaluations that suggest possible causes but no remedies or that recommend further study have limited use in the legislative process.

Evaluation intended for legislative use must also be timely. Horizons for legislative action are dominated by the length of the legislative session and two-year election cycles. Some legislatures have commissioned long-term multiyear studies that allow extensive tracking of clients over time or observing control groups, but typically they require information more promptly to address what are considered immediate problems. In those cases, legislatures will act with the best information they have available, whether an evaluation is complete or not. For example, in the case concerning nursing home regulation, legislators introduced a bill to correct perceived problems but postponed action pending the evaluation results. Had the evaluation results not been available as the legislative session drew to a close, action on the bill would have proceeded, and the evaluation, when finally completed, would not have been used. Consequently the research methodologies chosen for an evaluation are often influenced by the time available, and decisions are often based on discussions between evaluators and legislators about legislative schedules and the type of information that can be made available.

In each of the three evaluations described, evaluators designed their studies after discussions with legislators on the range of questions that needed to be addressed, the expectations legislators had of the programs or agencies, and the timetable within which legislative action would occur. As a result of these design considerations, each evaluation played a central role in legislative and management changes to the programs.

References

"Prudent Call for Added Vigilance at Investment Board." *Milwaukee Journal Sentinel* (editorial), July 14, 1995, p. 10A.
Shulha, L., and Cousins, B. "Evaluation Use: Theory, Research, and Practice Since 1986." *Evaluation Practice,* 1997, *18* (3).
Wohlstetter, P. "The Politics of Legislative Evaluations: Fire Alarm and Police Patrol as Oversight Procedures." *Evaluation Practice,* 1990, *11* (1).
Zahn, M., and Umhoefer, D. "Questionable Care." *Milwaukee Journal Sentinel,* Mar. 2–6, 1997.

DON BEZRUKI *is program evaluation director of the Wisconsin Legislative Audit Bureau.*

JANICE MUELLER *is the state auditor of Wisconsin.*

KAREN MCKIM *is a senior project supervisor at the Wisconsin Legislative Audit Bureau.*

Studies of privatization, including case studies, provide lessons on how to embark on privatization efforts, but they may not be predictive of the cost-saving potential for individual jurisdictions. Redirecting and improving on how the questions about privatization are asked can help to provide more useful information to policymakers.

Lessons Learned from Evaluating the Feasibility of Privatizing Government Services

Robert C. Thomas, Kathy Gookin, Beth Keating, Valerie Whitener

As the policy debate over privatization continues and remains especially tense in sensitive areas such as corrections, program evaluators are faced with the reality that support for privatization is increasing among state governments. And as might be expected, interest in cost savings is a major driver of this trend (Chi and Jasper, 1997, pp. 4–5).

In 1995 Washington's state legislature asked its Joint Legislative Audit and Review Committee (JLARC) to study the feasibility of privatizing adult prison facilities. More recently JLARC revisited the issues of privatization in an evaluation of the potential for managed competition for highways maintenance functions. Study team members have also participated and represented the state legislature as neutral parties in seminars and workshops sponsored by the U.S. Department of Justice, the National Conference of State Legislatures, and the National Institute of Justice.

We were members of the JLARC teams assigned to these studies. We were fortunate that other states and jurisdictions, by taking the first steps, had provided us with useful information and, in two instances, with case studies. The situation henceforth for other program evaluators will be similar. As more privatization occurs, evaluations of those experiences can serve to inform future policy decisions.

This chapter covers the major lessons learned from JLARC's work, describes some useful tools and guidelines for those who are involved in privatization efforts, and suggests areas for further evaluation. Although several of the sections that follow provide information on what should be done in the event that a state decides to pursue privatization, this should not be understood as an endorsement of privatization on our part or of JLARC.

Identifying the Research Question

Before we discuss the approach we took in our studies of privatization, it is important to point out a major distinction between the question we were trying to answer and the questions that are more typically posed when the issue of privatization is raised. The questions "*Will* privatization save money?" and "*Does* privatization save money?" are often heard. These were essentially the questions that the Government Accounting Office (GAO) sought to answer in a report that has been widely disseminated and hotly debated (GAO, 1996). The impetus for the report was Congress's interest in whether there should be increased privatization of correctional facilities in the federal Bureau of Prisons. GAO attempted to answer these questions by reviewing selected cost comparison studies published since 1991.

Posed in such broad terms, GAO's answer to the first question (*Will* privatization save money?) was bound to be the following: "We could not conclude from these studies that privatization of correctional facilities will not save money" (GAO, 1996). The problem with the question was that any lack of conclusiveness in any of the studies, or any examples of studies that reached different conclusions, would predetermine the answer. GAO's answer to the second question (*Does* privatization save money?) was that "studies do not offer substantial evidence that savings have occurred" (GAO, 1996). This answer was equally unelucidating because it was based on the notion that if there are conflicting results from different studies, the answer must necessarily be inconclusive. GAO made no attempt to determine independently whether savings or additional costs in the state examples under review had actually occurred.

The question we were faced with was more relevant to our audience and susceptible to being answered in a practical manner: "*Can* privatization save money, and if so, what can be done to ensure that the savings are realized?" We applied this approach to one of the preaudit questions in our prisons study: "How can Washington address existing constitutional, statutory, or labor barriers to privatization?" If we had asked instead, "Is privatization of prisons legal in Washington?" the study would never have been conducted, because the short answer was no. There were statutory prohibitions to contracting out work that had been traditionally done by civil service employees. Fortunately attorneys from the state's Office of the Attorney General provided legal analysis for JLARC on how to mitigate the legal problems. Not only did this analysis indicate needed changes in statute, should Washington choose to embark on privatization, but it also offered advice on how to avoid unconstitutional delegation of power and overcome constraints from collective bargaining. Our report (JLARC, 1996) presents the attorneys' solutions in detail. Some of the solutions may be applicable to other jurisdictions, and we thus refer readers who are interested in these legal matters to the report. In the remainder of this chapter, we focus on the more general questions regarding cost savings.

Cost Savings Potential from Privatization

In efforts to address the issue of potential savings from privatization, we combined two approaches: reviews of existing studies and detailed case studies.

Reviews of Existing Studies on Prison Privatization. In our review of the literature on prison privatization, we found numerous published sources that debate the pros and cons of privatization, but there were relatively few studies by academic researchers that attempted to compare costs (Urban Institute, 1989; Logan and McGriff, 1989; Sellers, 1989). We found that we could not use these studies to draw any general conclusions about the potential for cost savings for prisons through privatization. The problems with these studies are that they either did not compare well-matched facilities or they relied on hypothetical scenarios. This is not a criticism of those studies, because the authors had to rely on the very limited experiences with prison privatization of a decade ago. There is much more experience now.

We also reviewed cost studies from other states. The most important of these have been recent attempts to set cost benchmarks for targeted savings from privatization. The way this works is that states either estimate what the public costs would be of operating a particular new facility, or they identify their current costs of operating similar prisons within their system. Through a Request for Proposals (RFP), private companies are asked to respond with proposals that would result in a minimum cost-savings percentage (such as 7 to 10 percent) compared to the benchmark. If the benchmarks are accurately and appropriately estimated and the state receives responsive bids, then the compensation provided for in the contracts, compared to the benchmark, should indicate an amount of savings to be expected from privatization.

Two years before our study on prison privatization (JLARC, 1996), we had gained experience in estimating the costs of prison operations. In *Department of Corrections Capacity Planning and Implementation* (JLARC, 1994), we had identified facility operating costs by security level in order to determine if some of the most inefficient prison facilities should be replaced. The findings from the report led to legislative approval of several capital projects intended to achieve operational savings.

Based on this experience, and knowing the care that must go into establishing benchmarks, we were reluctant to accept projected savings based on benchmarks at face value. Unfortunately the time frame for the study did not allow for the extent of review that would have enabled us to say in most cases whether recent benchmarking efforts in other states are likely to result in savings. This is an area where independent research by program evaluators could provide valuable cost information and lessons learned that could be of significant importance for future decisions regarding privatization.

Review of Studies on Maintenance Contracting and Managed Competition. Nearly all state and Canadian provincial highway and transportation agencies, as well as many counties and cities, contract for some portion of their highway maintenance work, although practices vary widely. The amount contracted ranges from none in Puerto Rico to 100 percent in Wisconsin and British Columbia. Therefore it is not surprising that there is a rich body of studies that compare the costs of public and private highway maintenance activities.

In a performance audit of Washington's Highways and Rail Programs (JLARC, 1998), Cambridge Systematics, Inc., consultants to JLARC, focused on recent studies from several states, one city, and an internal study conducted for the Washington State Department of Transportation. Each of the highways maintenance studies suggested that the contracting entities had reduced costs or improved services. The Massachusetts experience was given the most prominence in the report because there had been two independent reviews, one by scholars (Gow and others, 1993) and one by an accounting firm (Coopers and Lybrand, 1996), that confirmed the increased service levels and cost savings. The Massachusetts experience was also of interest because it has engaged in managed competition. The idea behind managed competition is to create an environment that injects market dynamics into government services in an attempt to achieve quality at the lowest cost. Private sector bids are solicited for a service, such as highway maintenance, and are then compared to a bid prepared by the agency workforces currently performing the service.

After the review of the Massachusetts and other studies, the question remained whether Washington could expect to achieve savings through managed competition and increased privatization. Currently Washington contracts only 2 percent of its maintenance due to statutory constraints. A difficulty in trying to predict what the state's experience might be with more contracting is that it is unknown how efficient Washington is in comparison to the states that have reported cost savings.

JLARC addressed this issue by reviewing the results of a study conducted on behalf of the Washington State Transportation Commission (Conrad, Nelson, and Jones, 1993). Maintenance districts within the Department of Transportation participated in the study on a "shadow" approach. This allowed the Department of Transportation to identify projects, prepare in-house bids, call for bids from contractors, track agency costs for completing the projects, and then compare the results. However, in response to labor concerns and the state's current contracting legal restrictions, no projects could actually be awarded to private contractors. A number of cities and counties also participated in the pilot and were allowed to award contracts to private contractors. The potential savings identified from the maintenance projects were estimated by the department to be in the 8 to 10 percent range and were judged to be a realistic expectation should constraints to managed competition be removed.

The performance audit recommended that a pilot project for managed competition be implemented, provided the legislature would pass the necessary enabling legislation. Crucial to the success of the pilot project would be the ability of the state to identify accurately and understand its own costs. As a recent GAO report on privatization stated, "Reliable and complete cost data on government activities are needed to ensure a sound competitive process and to assess overall performance. Reliable and complete data. . . simplify privatization decisions and make these decisions easier to implement and justify to potential critics" (GAO, 1997).

Case Studies of Prison Privatization. JLARC performance auditors conducted case studies of Louisiana and Tennessee to ascertain whether savings from privatization are possible. The case study approach was chosen after it was determined that the available published cost comparisons had significant limitations or methodological weaknesses.

Louisiana and Tennessee were selected because these two states have had the most experience with privatization, and each has privately and publicly run facilities that are identical in design and capacity. These two factors are critical to analyzing labor costs, which account for the majority of prison budgets. From previous work (JLARC, 1994), we know that controlling for design and capacity will facilitate better comparisons of custody staffing. Controlling for design and capacity also allows for better comparison of support services and management between prisons. Although these latter two cost centers are usually less sensitive, say, to scale than custody staffing, we have found that they do vary between facilities and among states.

JLARC's review of data provided by Louisiana and Tennessee suggest that these two states have achieved moderate savings of up to 4 to 6 percent on a per-inmate basis. At the same time, our review of private company expenses suggests that the private companies were still able to make sizable profits. Our analysis of incidence reports and on-site visits by correctional professionals from the Washington Department of Corrections revealed no major differences among the facilities in terms of quality of programs and services or threats to public safety. A more recent study of the same facilities in Louisiana by Louisiana State University (LSU) (Archambeault and Deis, 1996) has estimated savings to the state in the range of 12 to 14 percent. The most recent effort to reconcile the differences between the estimates of the two studies suggests that the JLARC report may have slightly understated the public facility's costs, while the LSU study appears to have substantially overstated the public facility's costs ("Private Prisons . . . ," 1998).

Of particular interest to the Washington State legislature was the issue of how private companies could reportedly operate at lower costs and still produce enough of a profit to stay in business. The information gleaned from the two case studies provided answers that were not particularly surprising.

Personnel comprise approximately 70 percent of operating costs in the state-run facilities we evaluated. Among all the areas where there exist opportunities for private firms to save money, personnel is clearly the area that has the most potential. For the three private facilities examined in our case studies, we estimated that the number of staff ranged from 88 to 97 percent of state facilities staffing and that the average salaries for those personnel ranged from 69 to 93 percent of state salaries.

The magnitude of the potential for savings in the area of personnel can be shown in an example. If a private facility can operate with 90 percent of state staffing and at 85 percent of average state salaries, this translates into personnel savings of 24 percent. Since personnel costs comprise about 70 percent of all operating costs, this results in a savings to the total budget of approximately 16 percent. Some of the savings are passed on to the state to the extent that the contracted per diems for the private facilities are less than the state's per diems. The example shows, however, that personnel can be a major source of profit for the private companies.

From our site visits and reviews of staffing patterns, two general explanations emerged for how the private firms achieve these staff and salary savings. First, there is a greater tendency for staff to have responsibilities in more than one area and for management staff to have responsibilities in several areas. Second, more flexibility in the use of staff, including corrections officers, results in fewer staff (or less overtime, or both) needed to cover mandatory posts. We did not find that the private firms paid less in benefits, such as health care and retirement.

The two case studies provided answers to some of the legislature's questions, but it would be problematic to generalize from the experience of these two states regarding the potential for cost savings. Although the case studies indicate that savings from privatization are possible, they do not provide good estimates of the range of potential savings for other states, for several reasons.

Both states designed and built the facilities used in the comparison, which means that the private companies were not in a position to achieve potential savings through lower development costs had they built the facilities or through differences in design that might lower operating costs. Proponents of prison privatization argue that the maximum potential for savings comes when private companies have the opportunity to design and build the facilities they will operate. For this reason, Florida and Puerto Rico have recently taken the approach of soliciting bids under the comprehensive approach. This raises an issue, however, over how to compare the operational and capital costs components of competing bids. For jurisdictions that are interested in considering this approach, the JLARC report (JLARC, 1996) offers a methodology for making such a comparison.

Furthermore, how much a state might save through contracting will depend on several factors. An important one is how efficient (how good a benchmark) the public operation is before embarking on privatization or managed competition. If a state operation is inefficient, then the private operators are presented with an easy target to beat. Thus, the experience of a state that has inefficient operations will suggest little for a state with efficient operations.

And no matter how efficient or inefficient a state's operations are, the accuracy of estimates of how much a state may be saving through privatization or managed competition depends entirely on how well the state has appropriately identified its fixed and variable costs. As the examples of the JLARC and LSU case studies of Louisiana have shown, arriving at a best estimate of actual costs, and the costs that can be avoided with privatization, is a difficult task, and errors are always possible.

A final limitation of the case studies relates to a situation that is inherent in the contracting relationship. From the information we were able to obtain from the two private companies that operate facilities in Tennessee and Louisiana, these companies were able to offer cost reductions to the states and at the same time make a profit. If the states had been armed with the same information we had been able to gather (which they are in a position to do now), they potentially could have used this information in contract negotiations to gain greater cost savings for themselves at the expense of the companies' profits.

General Guidelines

Our role as staff that conducts research and performance audits for a legislative body is to present what is feasible and to offer information on best practices should the legislature decide to pursue privatization.

The result of our case studies, and the limitations of such a methodology, is that savings estimates from any state, no matter how accurate, do not serve to demonstrate what the experience of another state will be. They do, however, offer the possibility that transferable practices might exist to improve a state's chances of generating savings. We found that much depends on the care that was taken in estimating the state's costs, designing the RFP, possibly setting a target for savings, choosing a contractor, and then negotiating, executing, and monitoring the contract. The ability of a private company to operate a prison differently from a public facility depends on the degree of flexibility allowed to the private firm under the contract. Ultimately even if a private facility can operate for less, the state would not necessarily capture any of these savings for itself unless it received responsive bids with per diem costs lower than its own.

From the lessons learned in our evaluations of the feasibility of privatizing government operations, we identified eight general guidelines, or implementation steps, that can be followed to minimize risk associated with privatization while promoting cost savings without sacrificing quality:

1. *Develop a business strategy* that reflects the objectives of the state service's various stakeholders. An important part of developing a business strategy would be to identify not only the functions that could be competitively bid but also the core functions that the state should retain due to constitutional constraints or in the interests of protecting the public.
2. *Propose and implement authorizing legislation* that ensures that all options are available and that they are considered fairly and equitably.
3. *Implement reliable cost accounting systems* to enable adequate tracking and comparison of costs.

4. *Develop transition strategies and resources* to assist management and labor to adopt more cost-effective business practices.

5. *Develop RFPs* that set a minimum cost-saving target that must be met for proposals to be considered responsive. Requests for proposals should set standards for programs, operations, and facility design and construction defined as what should be provided and should allow respondents to be flexible and creative in how to meet those standards.

6. *Use the RFP process to develop and implement a pilot project* to test the feasibility of the new approach. The results of the pilot should be used to fine-tune the approach prior to rolling out the new contracting methodology on a broader basis.

7. *Establish performance monitoring and oversight* to ensure that the new contracting processes result in the expected outcomes. This will be necessary to help ensure that the government's interests are protected and that accountability of both the state agencies and private contractors is maintained.

8. *Develop a contingency plan* for the smooth transition of operations from one private vendor to another, or to the state, in the event of contract expiration or termination.

These guidelines will help to ensure that a level playing field will exist in a system of managed competition so that all cost-effective resource alternatives can be seriously considered.

Given all of the variables, we would not agree with those who would endorse privatization based on the assumption that states necessarily will benefit from more cost-effective private operations (Archambeault and Deis, 1996, p. 573). From our reviews of highway maintenance studies and the two prison case studies, we have found evidence that the introduction of competition into areas that have previously been government monopolies does afford an opportunity to reduce costs and improve service and, if done properly, can be accomplished while minimizing risk.

References

Archambeault, W. G., and Deis, D. R., Jr. *Cost Effectiveness Comparisons of Private Versus Public Prisons in Louisiana: A Comprehensive Analysis of Allen, Avoyelles, and Winn Correctional Centers, Phase I (Revised)*. Baton Rouge: Louisiana State University, 1996.

Chi, K. S., and Jasper, C. *Private Practices: A Review of Privatization in State Government*. Lexington, Ky.: Council of State Governments, 1997.

Conrad, J. F., Nelson, P., and Jones, K. "The PCEM Approach to Privatization in the Washington State Department of Transportation." Paper 93–0763 presented at the annual meeting of the Transportation Research Board, Jan. 1993.

Coopers and Lybrand L.L.P. *Independent Assessment of Massachusetts Highway Maintenance Privatization Program*. Prepared for the Massachusetts Executive Office of Transportation and Construction, June 1996.

General Accounting Office. *Private and Public Prisons: Studies Comparing Operational Costs and/or Quality of Service*. GAO/CCD–96–158. Washington, D.C.: U.S. General Accounting Office, Aug. 1996.

General Accounting Office. *Privatization: Lessons Learned by State and Local Governments.* GAO/CCD–97–48. Washington, D.C.: U.S. General Accounting Office, Mar. 1997.

Gow, D., Jovicich, C., Laws, M., McLeod, S., Kakowka, S., Markovich, P. *From Public to Private: The Massachusetts Experience, 1991–1993.* Cambridge, Mass.: John F. Kennedy School of Government, Harvard University, Apr. 1993.

Joint Legislative Audit and Review Committee. *Department of Corrections Capacity Planning and Implementation.* Olympia, Wash.: Joint Legislative Audit and Review Committee, Jan. 1994.

Joint Legislative Audit and Review Committee. *Department of Corrections Privatization Feasibility Study.* Olympia, Wash.: Joint Legislative Audit and Review Committee, Jan.1996.

Joint Legislative Audit and Review Committee. *Department of Transportation Highways and Rail Programs Performance Audit, Proposed Final Report.* Olympia, Wash.: Joint Legislative Audit and Review Committee, Mar. 1998.

Logan, C. H., and McGriff, B. W. *Comparing Costs of Public and Private Prisons: A Case Study.* National Institute of Justice Report No. 216. Washington, D.C.: National Institute of Justice, Sept.–Oct. 1989.

"Private Prisons in the United States: An Assessment of Current Practice." Abt Associates Inc., Appendix I, pp. 8-13. Cambridge, Mass., 1998.

Sellers, M. P. "Private and Public Prisons: A Comparison of Costs, Programs and Facilities." *International Journal of Offender Therapy and Comparative Criminology,* 1989, 33 (3).

Thomas, R. C. Letter to William G. Archambeault, Louisiana State University, Mar. 7, 1997.

Urban Institute. *Comparison of Privately and Publicly Operated Corrections Facilities in Kentucky and Massachusetts.* Washington, D.C.: Urban Institute, Aug. 1989.

ROBERT C. THOMAS *is the principal management auditor supervisor for Washington State's Joint Legislative Audit and Review Committee (JLARC).*

KATHY GOOKIN *is a principal management auditor for Washington State's JLARC.*

BETH KEATING *is a principal management auditor for Washington State's JLARC.*

VALERIE WHITENER *is a management auditor for Washington State's JLARC.*

Statutes generally provide legislative program evaluation agencies with virtually unlimited access to information on programs supported with state funds.

Access to Information: The Legislative Advantage

R. Kirk Jonas

For a legislature to know whether the agencies and programs it funds are operating in an efficient, effective, and economical manner, legislative evaluators must have access to information sufficient to make such determinations. Consequently legislatures have generally afforded LPEs the right to examine any level of record held by an agency or program funded with state money. The theoretical question of access is often simply and directly addressed by statute. The question then becomes, How is access achieved from an operational standpoint? The right to examine individual records must be combined with the ability to do so.

Legislative evaluators must often combine access to information with considerable research resources. For example, a JLARC study team in 1997 completed a study of the implementation of the Comprehensive Services Act (CSA), a state-funded, locally administered program for at-risk youth. Because no central data existed on this program, the study mandate was fulfilled by conducting extensive site visits to local programs all over the state. The review was based on a systematic survey of 1,144 client records, many of them several hundred pages long and spread across various agencies. Although some were automated, the data were in separate databases that could not be accurately linked. Literally hundreds of person-days of site visits were involved. The availability of resources for extensive access to such sensitive records and the ability to use them add considerable richness to LPE research and value to the overall field of program evaluation.

Virginia's JLARC is not alone in its access to sensitive information. Legislative program evaluators and auditors in other states are usually granted extensive access to information of almost every type. This access has its basis in both the statutes of the various states and federal law and regulation. For example,

U.S. Department of Health and Human Services regulations on the confidentiality of alcohol and drug abuse patient records contain these provisions:

> The regulations permit disclosure without patient consent if the disclosure is to medical personnel to meet any individual's bona fide medical emergency (§ 2.51) or to qualified personnel for research (§2.52) audit, or program evaluation (§2.53). Qualified personnel may not include patient identifying information in any report or otherwise disclose patient identities except back to the program which was the source of the information (§§2–52[b] and 2.53[d]) [*Federal Register*, 1987].

An example of an extremely strong state statute is provided by Kansas. The Kansas Legislative Division of Post Audit has virtually unlimited access to information held by state agencies and entities funded by the state. In 1992 the division performed a study of health regulatory boards' programs for impaired medical providers (Legislative Division of Post Audit, 1993). The boards that had the information about impaired providers within their professions vigorously opposed providing it to the Division of Post Audit. They argued that the information had been obtained on the presumption of confidentiality. Further, some programs were intervention oriented, such as assisting a substance-dependent physician. The boards were afraid that providing access to such information theoretically could discourage future participation in the program.

The legislative post-auditor met with officials of all the regulatory boards. She stressed both the legal basis of the division's right to access, as well as its perfect record of preserving confidentiality. Ultimately the division was granted access to all the records it sought. Nevertheless, as a statement of principle, several officials in the health regulatory boards resigned to protest the disclosure of the information. This example underscores the differences in perspective that can be applied to the access issue.

Although virtually all LPE organizations have statutes providing access to information, the Kansas Legislative Division of Post Audit has an unusually powerful tool for ensuring that agencies comply. The auditor has the authority to direct the state's controller to stop payments to an agency or fund-receiving entity that refuses to provide requested information. This provision is a powerful motivator for compliance (Hinton, 1998).

The Virginia JLARC has neither subpoena power nor the power to cut off funds. These tools have not proved necessary, however; JLARC ultimately has received access to all of the data it has ever sought. The Virginia General Assembly has been a strong supporter of the oversight function, and state agencies are aware of this commitment. In addition to JLARC's standing statutes on access, assembly language in specific study resolutions and budget amendments directing studies underscore the staff's access to information.

Along with the considerable access afforded legislative evaluators comes a profound responsibility not to abuse this access. Individuals' records (whether tax, client, or patient) must be carefully protected both during and after the study process. Study findings must be generalized and identities carefully protected. Virginia statute permits this by making many JLARC records exempt from the state's Freedom of Information Act. Sometimes a finding of importance must go unreported because it is impossible to report without revealing the identity of an individual. Finally, strict archival procedures must be developed so that records integrity is preserved both during a study and after its completion.

The implications of the availability of such records to the larger evaluation audience are substantial. Legislative program evaluators represent a source of information that is often not elsewhere available. In seeking source material on public policy issues, the evaluation field should be cognizant of the rich resources available through LPE offices.

Creation of Databases

Data needed to fulfill study mandates do not always exist and sometimes must be created to address adequately the legislature's need for information. Two recent JLARC studies, a 1997 study of the Comprehensive Services Act and an ongoing study of welfare reform, demonstrate both LPE access to information and the legislature's willingness to devote sufficient resources to collect the information.

Review of the Comprehensive Services Act. When the 1992 Virginia General Assembly enacted legislation to provide comprehensive services to at-risk children with serious behavioral and emotional problems, it was responding to a fragmented system that was ineffective in the delivery of services and administratively inefficient. The CSA combined resources from a variety of funding streams and empowered localities to pool resources flexibly in what was hoped to be a cost-effective, client-friendly manner. Localities were given the ability to coordinate and direct resources to programs they felt best met the needs of at-risk children in their communities. Lawmakers expected this approach would both save money and better serve children.

Despite initial optimism regarding the program, early experience indicated that cost increases were not being constrained. Further, it was unclear whether delivery of services was more effective or efficient than it had been. Ultimately the study found that "the primary factor responsible for the expansion of CSA is the growth in the State's at risk population. . . . Similarly, much of the local variation that exists in the costs of serving a given participant in the program can be explained by the level of dysfunction present in the child" (JLARC, 1998). The development of such findings was a critical step in the understanding of this complex, devolved program. To reach this point, however, JLARC staff had to spend several person-years developing a database from confidential juvenile records.

Extensive reviews of confidential client files were required. The team used or developed a number of data collection instruments to extract information from juvenile files on such subjects as severity of psychiatric illness, family background, and criminal behavior. Table 4.1, from the report, illustrates the richness of these data sources in providing information on the effects of CSA-funded intervention. Pre- and postintervention behaviors of juveniles could be generalized from the study approach.

The sensitivity of the case-specific information can be remarkable, as demonstrated by the following case example, one of several used to illustrate characteristics of juvenile participants served through the CSA (pseudonyms are used in all case examples):

> John was referred to CSA by the juvenile court in April of 1994. At the time of his referral, John was 14 years of age, was the product of a severely dysfunctional family, had lived a traumatic life, and had a serious criminal record. The social history report on John indicated that he was kidnapped by his father at age 4. For eight years, he lived on the run with his father, until he was abandoned at the North Carolina Department of Social Services. More significantly, during these eight years, John was repeatedly raped and physically abused by his father. Medically, he has tested positive for numerous head traumas which may have been the result of physical abuse.
>
> When John was finally returned to his mother, his living conditions only marginally improved. His mother was in poor health with cancer of the brain, liver, and pancreas. In addition, the social history reports that her parenting skills were negligible due mostly to her family background, which was characterized by chronic alcoholic parents, extensive drug use, court involvement, and serious

Table 4.1. Pre- and Post-CSA Criminal Behavior of Juveniles, JLARC Study Sample

Juvenile Criminal Record Prior to Receiving CSA Services		Percentage of Youth, Based on the Nature of the Crime Committed Since Receiving Services				
Most Serious Crime Committed	Percentage of Youths	No Post-CSA Crimes	Felony Against Person	Other Felonies	Misdemeanors	Status and Other Offenses
No Criminal Record	86	86	1	3	8	2
Felony Against Person	4	46	18	9	20	7
Other Felonies	3	12	21	24	40	3
Misdemeanors	5	56	0	9	23	12
Status and Other Offenses	2	63	0	4	20	12

Note: Reported relationships are statistically significant at a .01 level of significance. However, because 64 percent of the cells have counts fewer than five, chi-square may not be a valid test. A total of 747 cases were examined for criminal records data.

Source: JLARC staff analysis of data collected from CSA participant files.

physical abuse. At the time John was returned to his mother, she was living in an apartment with no furniture. All of the members of the household—John, his mother, aunt, and sister—slept on the floor. Unable to work because of her illness, John's mother relied on SSI [supplemental security income] and AFDC [Aid to Families with Dependent Children] payments for support. Her total income from these sources was $9,540 a year [JLARC, 1998, p. 32].

This case study is rich in specific, accurate information, and it has been adapted to conceal the identities of the individuals involved. Through an institutional exposure process, all Virginia JLARC reports are released to appropriate agencies for factual verification and review prior to their public release. Thus, sensitive cases such as this one are reviewed by the affected agency prior to the public release of the information. At times, modifications to case studies may be made if the agency has confidentiality concerns.

Studying Welfare Reform. Like many other states, Virginia implemented a comprehensive system of welfare reform in the mid-1990s. Phased in prior to federal welfare reform through a waiver granted by the U.S. Department of Health and Human Services, the Virginia General Assembly believed that sufficient time had elapsed to evaluate the effects of the new program. As with the CSA program, however, welfare reform in Virginia has been a state and local cooperative effort, and central sources of data have not been sufficient to provide needed information or address important legislative concerns. To develop needed information, staff have visited twenty-one participating localities and collected data on client history and behavior. A total of 2,511 client files, about two inches thick, have been reviewed. Information has been collected on a wide array of topics, including the history of clients' participation in the welfare system, the flow of participants through the system (by an examination of case logs), and barriers to employment. Data from this comprehensive review were coded onto a twenty-one–page data collection instrument. The information, collected from confidential client files, will provide generalizable information on program implementation and client outcomes associated with welfare reform.

Welfare reform is a largely devolved program, with the federal Aid to Families with Dependent Children (AFDC) program being replaced by a wide range of state-based Temporary Aid to Needy Families (TANF) programs. While AFDC permitted states some flexibility, TANF (and the other package of programs which constitute "welfare") is much more decentralized. It is conceivable that future evaluations of this highly devolved program will require the increased participation of state evaluation units.

Access to Tax Records

Few other government records are as closely held as federal, state, and local tax records. Even candidates for the office of president of the United States appear to have been largely successful in determining for themselves whether their federal income tax records become public. Virginia has safeguards within its system that limit the access of even Department of Taxation employees to certain records. Nonetheless, access to tax records is essential if a legislative evaluation agency is to study a department of taxation. In 1991 the general assembly directed JLARC to study the Virginia Department of Taxation as part of a series of studies on Virginia's budgeting process. This study presented two problems in terms of access to information: the inherently private nature of individual and corporate income tax returns and agency reluctance to cooperate on any level.

The confidentiality of individual tax records is something that is (and should be) taken very seriously by state departments of taxation. Consequently the Virginia Department of Taxation was understandably reluctant to allow legislative evaluators access to these records. Only after extensive discussions with both JLARC and the Internal Revenue Service and study of state statutes did the department grant JLARC staff access to individual and corporate tax records.

JLARC staff reviewed numerous records, focusing especially on opportunities for the department to increase compliance with tax policy and, consequently, increase collections. By examining records selected for audit, JLARC was able to determine that a state tax gap (the difference in the amount the state would receive if it collected all taxes owed and the amount actually received) of approximately one-half billion dollars existed. This gap was extremely important because Virginia had experienced a billion-dollar revenue shortfall in 1990. Examination of records was essential to the study because the department's representation of its audit sampling techniques was not accurate.

Another finding of the study was revealed by the examination of thirty files of accepted compromise offers. This review illustrated the extensive discretion the tax commissioner exercised in abating (essentially forgiving) taxes due the commonwealth. The following example was used to illustrate the finding that for twenty-three of the thirty files reviewed, "the only evidence of doubtful collectibility was the information provided by the taxpayer in the letter to the department" (JLARC, 1992, p. 100). The example also illustrates how a specific record can be laundered to make a point without disclosing confidential information.

> A taxpayer submitted a compromise offer of approximately $11,000 for an individual income tax liability of approximately $55,000. The acceptance of the offer noted that "information available indicates doubtful collectibility exists." However, the only source of information in the file was the taxpayer's letter. The letter stated that the taxpayer's children would borrow money to pay the amount of the offer. The letter also stated that the taxpayer had no other financial resources, and that a financial statement was enclosed. However, the file did not contain a financial statement or any other financial information concerning the taxpayer. Therefore, the financial information used by the department as the basis for determining doubtful collectibility could not be verified [JLARC, 1992, p. 100].

This case study was disguised somewhat in order to screen the identity of the taxpayer while still clearly making the point. As part of JLARC's report exposure process, the example was reviewed by the department prior to its public release. JLARC staff adopted some of the suggestions of the department (such as deleting a reference to the taxpayer's occupation) to ensure the confidentiality of the taxpayer. As a practice, staff did not make copies of taxpayer records but reviewed them at the department. After the study, these notes were destroyed.

Another access issue encountered during JLARC's study of the Department of Taxation was agency reluctance to cooperate. This is not uncommon when JLARC studies the organization and management of a state agency. Agencies sometimes request that supervisors sit in on interviews to ensure (from their perspective) that the information provided is accurate. The effect of such a practice would be to intimidate the employee. The Department of Taxation was one of the agencies that JLARC studied that wanted to have a supervisor sit in on interviews. JLARC rejected this approach, and ultimately the secretary of finance directed the tax commissioner to allow private interviews. Even after that directive, however, department managers circulated a memorandum advising departmental staff that "the Commissioner wants this review tightly controlled." A later memo coached departmental staff on how to perform in "one-on-one" interviews:

> Often an experienced interviewer will use a technique known as the "interviewer pause." This is a period of silence after a question is answered. This "pause" places pressure on the interviewee to say or comment in order to break the silence. Please watch for this. Do not add to the initial request for information. Simply wait for the next question [JLARC, 1992, p. 23].

It also became apparent that surveys sent to employees through interoffice mail were subject to monitoring by department management. JLARC's response was to mail surveys on departmental management and morale directly to the employees, using first-class mail for delivery and return of the surveys. Thus, a supervisor who attempted to interfere with the survey would be violating U.S. postal laws.

No doubt some of the obstacles that departmental officials raised are motivated by a concern for the sanctity of their records; nevertheless, a good evaluator will insist on full access to needed records. If anything, agency strategies to impede evaluations almost always backfire. Such efforts generally motivate evaluation staff to look harder and can provoke departmental employees to volunteer more information.

Access to Data in Private Companies

One of the quiet revolutions of American public policy has been the privatization of public functions. Privatization itself is not a new concept. Private operation of toll roads, bridges, and the like preceded the republic itself. Private contractors have made billions of dollars off Medicaid and the space program.

Most states have long used private contractors to build the majority of roads in their highway systems. Private correctional facilities are no longer viewed as an innovative oddity. More recently, private companies, such as Maximus and Lockheed Martin, have moved into the delivery of social service programs. As the line blurs between what is public and what is proprietary, the importance of access to information for evaluation purposes takes on new importance.

Without access to private vendor information, states cannot adequately exercise the oversight function. It may be reasonable to expect that most contractors operate honorably and fulfill their contracts to the best of their ability; nevertheless, there will be instances of fraud or nonperformance. Union soldiers during the Civil War discovered that even the noblest of causes did not prevent some contractors from behaving dishonorably. Cardboard soles on boots provided by contractors dissolved soon after they were accepted by the army and issued to soldiers. To protect against abuses and ensure that the taxpayers' money is not wasted by bureaucrats or private contractors, legislative program evaluators must have access to records of private companies doing state business.

On a 1997 study of adult care residences, JLARC staff needed to inspect the care that residents received that was subsidized by state funds. Initially home operators were reluctant to let JLARC staff enter their facilities. In fact, some denied entry even to state case managers. To overcome this reluctance, staff used several strategies, in addition to the assertion of JLARC's legal right. Staff contacted the association representing adult care residences and reviewed the study approach with them. The association publicized the study, emphasizing its potential for influencing an increase in state aid. Further, staff generally arranged to visit residences with the Department of Social Services licensing staff. These approaches resulted in full access to the private residences.

Access to the proprietary information of private companies can also be an issue. JLARC's right to access to proprietary information was raised as an issue during a 1992 study of the state's Center for Innovative Technology and again during a 1993 study of the Virginia Retirement System's investment in the RF&P Corporation. In both cases, access to needed information was ultimately granted.

In the review of the Virginia Retirement System, JLARC needed to examine the system's investment in the RF&P Corporation, a real estate company in which the retirement system owned all of the stock. JLARC staff gained access to company documents and to confidential meetings of the board of directors by agreeing to sign nondisclosure agreements. The agreements set out how information about the company would be used, who would have access to the information collected, how the information would be stored, and how it would be destroyed upon completion of the audit.

In some cases access to proprietary information may be limited. In a review of the state computer center, for example, the JLARC staff hired a firm to complete a benchmarking analysis. The benchmarking methodology was proprietary, limiting staff access to the details of the analysis. In this case, staff concluded that the limitation did not pose a problem because of wide industry acceptance of the benchmark as appropriate. Whenever such limitations arise, however, the LPE agency will need to judge whether such limits jeopardize the soundness of the research.

Other Barriers to Access

Unfettered access to information is not easily won. Sometimes it is not denied so much as delayed. For example, most delays in accessing needed information frequently come at the beginning of a new gubernatorial administration. During the 1994–1998 administration, Virginia's governor replaced 75 percent of all state agency heads during the first year of his administration. The new agency heads, sensitive to the new governor's interests in managing information flow, were sometimes less than responsive to legislative information requests.

In such cases, the LPE organization is best served if it avoids being confrontational but persistently asserts its right to the information, assures the agency that the requested materials will be used responsibly, and convinces the agency that confidential records will remain confidential. The most persuasive argument (for Kansas as well as Virginia) is that the LPE organization has a perfect record for maintaining confidentiality. Executive agencies that have entrusted LPE organizations with sensitive data can be used as references to other executive agencies if confidentiality was maintained and records were handled appropriately.

An Emerging Issue: Who Pays for the Data?

On several recent studies, executive branch agencies have requested payment from JLARC staff for data requests. JLARC management has also received inquiries on its policy in this regard from other states, where similar requests have been made. The office's policy has always been that the agency being studied must provide data requested. In a June 10, 1998, letter to an agency head, the staff director of JLARC stated:

> I understand that you recently informed my staff that there will be some costs involved to fulfill JLARC's data request dated May 22, 1998, and that your staff is currently estimating that cost. I further understand that you inquired of my staff whether it is JLARC's practice to pay for data that it requests from State agencies during the course of evaluations. It is not our practice to make such payments.
>
> I do not believe that it is appropriate to charge a legislative oversight agency, which is mandated by the General Assembly to complete a performance audit, for access to data maintained by an executive branch agency. I look forward to the agency providing JLARC with the previously requested data in a timely fashion at no charge. Please feel free to contact me with any questions or comments you may have.

The requested data were forthcoming. The ability of legislative program evaluation units (and auditors) to perform their duties would be significantly impaired if these agencies were required to pay for data requests. Indeed, it is not difficult to imagine a scenario where agencies could prevent meaningful review by attaching prohibitive price tags to data. In the long run, it is unlikely that legislatures would permit this type of behavior by agencies. In the short run, however, it is possible that a few agencies could delay evaluations until a legislature took a definitive stand.

Disposal of Confidential Records

Safeguarding sensitive records is an important responsibility of LPE organizations. JLARC's records management policies are twenty-six pages long and require frequent revision, particularly because of technology issues, such as the disposal of computer databases. During the study process, JLARC records are generally classified as legislative working papers or investigative notes, and thus are exempt from the Freedom of Information Act. After a study has been briefed and printed, however, these classifications no longer apply, and study records are accessible to the public and press. If staff have been careless in classifying confidential records, inappropriate material could inadvertently be included with general archival material. Sensitive materials need to be identified as such, separated from open records, and stored separately in locked files during the study, and they must remain separate after the study. They should be scheduled for destruction soon after the study, and finally destroyed appropriately. A record of the destruction activity should be filed permanently.

Conclusion

In order to fulfill legislative study mandates, JLARC staff have been required to access a wide range of documents. On a few occasions, staff have encountered circumstances that dictated that they not accept sensitive information. During a recent study of the feasibility of converting Camp Pendleton (the military reservation of the Virginia National Guard) to a state park, JLARC staff were asked to sign confidentiality statements prior to a classified military briefing by the Navy SEALs command. (Camp Pendleton is adjacent to naval facilities that are used to practice beach landings and other military operations.) Rather than be informed of sensitive operations that could not be reported to the legislature, staff opted instead for an unclassified briefing. All of the staff's questions were addressed in this briefing, and there were no restrictions on the use of the information.

Having information that cannot be communicated to the legislature is of little value to LPE staff. Fortunately such occurrences are rare. In other cases, staff have signed confidentiality statements proposed by agencies, since the statements essentially provide that information would be used only in a generalized format. This is standard staff practice, but the statements provided an added level of assurance and comfort to agency personnel concerned about their own liability.

Access to information and the resources to create data sets from sensitive information provide legislative program evaluators with rich sources. The overall evaluation community cannot expect access comparable to that granted LPE organizations. Knowing that the foundations of legislative research are potentially very deep, however, should encourage the evaluation community to use such studies more often.

References

Federal Register, June 9, 1987, p. 21796.

Hinton, B. Interview, Jul. 23, 1998.

Joint Legislative Audit and Review Commission. *Review of the Comprehensive Services Act.* Richmond, Va.: Commonwealth of Virginia, Jan. 1998.

Joint Legislative Audit and Review Commission. *Services for Mentally Disabled Residents of Adult Care Residences.* Richmond, Va.: Commonwealth of Virginia, July 1997.

Joint Legislative Audit and Review Commission. *Review of the Department of Taxation.* Richmond, Va.: Commonwealth of Virginia, Jan. 1992.

Legislative Division of Post Audit. Reviewing Fee-Funded Regulatory Agencies' Programs for Impaired Licensees. Topeka, Ks.: Legislature of Kansas, Jan. 1993.

R. KIRK JONAS is deputy director of the Virginia Joint Legislative Audit and Review Commission of the Virginia General Assembly and an adjunct professor in the University of Richmond Department of Political Science.

The development of systems models for program evaluations provides unique benefits. Computer simulations can facilitate an understanding of multi-issue legislation and help policymakers reach comprehensive conclusions.

The Use of Systems Modeling in Legislative Program Evaluation

Patrick W. McIntire, Ann S. Glaze

Program evaluation for legislators is an emerging discipline that can provide valuable information to policymakers. Evaluators often face two fundamental problems, however: a lack of rigorous quantitative data on which to base defensible conclusions and recommendations, and a high degree of system complexity that precludes simple analyses (Stokey and Zeckhauser, 1978). Common quantitative tools for these studies rely on methodologies for social science research and associated statistical techniques (Weiss, 1977). Unfortunately, time, resources, and characteristics of agency data sets may not allow casual analyses that lead to meaningful conclusions and subsequent policy recommendations.

In addition, legislation is often comprehensive, so that several aspects of one or more agencies or issues are concurrently affected. Common evaluation techniques do not easily enable assessments of interactive and concurrent effects of these complex mandates. We investigated the use of systems modeling, or computer simulation, as one methodological tool to aid program evaluators when confronted by these circumstances.

Definition of Systems Modeling

Systems modeling is a dynamic process that realistically determines and joins important components of an organized body; the intent is to determine the behaviors of particular variables of interest over time using computer simulation. For example, a manufacturing business might model its overall production process by sequentially delineating and quantifying various components like raw materials, assembly rates, and shipping. Using appropriate software, one can connect these components, assign initial values, run the model, validate and determine the "behavior" of the model, and then evaluate the effects of one set of values.

Modeling analysts can incorporate two types of variables: those consisting of measured data, or hard variables, and those that are not measurable, at least for the moment, which we term soft variables. Analysts can reasonably quantify soft variables within the model, however, so that they interact mathematically within the system. The values of soft variables should be set relative to the behavior of the system as a whole and tempered by known characteristics. Determining these values can be an extensive exercise in itself. The capability to incorporate soft variables into these models is particularly advantageous when data are lacking, but their presence may preclude a rigorous and independent verification of the model itself. The proportions of hard and soft variables in the model must be considered when developing interpretations, conclusions, and recommendations.

Analysts can assess different management scenarios by changing important parameters in a systematic manner during subsequent simulations, that is, by performing experiments. Summarized results of these simulations allow policymakers to experience, conceptualize, and learn the effects of their decisions in a relatively safe manner (Morecroft, 1988). Analysts can compare alternative models in a similar fashion. Essentially the software calculates and tracks changes among all components within the system over a designated interval of time; it thereby offers a unique view of an organization not forthcoming with conventional techniques. Its use is based on establishing a reasonably realistic replication of the workings and interrelationships of the entity under study.

For legislative evaluation, analysts can test policy alternatives by changing one or two of the appropriate variables within the model and comparing these outcomes to those of the control model. Systems modeling as a research tool is occasionally used in other disciplines; for example, Cochrane, Kestle, Steinbok, Evans, and Heron (1995) forecast the costs of treatments for patients with ventriculoperitoneal shunts using a time-dependent cost analysis model that was developed with systems modeling software.

Building this perspective of a complex organization has several benefits. Foremost among these is an understanding of the functions and interrelationships among organizational, or system, components. With this knowledge, one can assess the effects of various management strategies, or policy recommendations, on one or more components or on the system as a whole; this capability is not forthcoming with conventional spreadsheet or statistical software. Of course, the value of this exercise directly relates to the quality of information on which the model is based. This quality must be honestly assessed and included in the interpretation of the model outcomes.

Unfortunately planners usually do not design public sector data systems to provide comprehensive program data. Computer capabilities more often evolve as a linear response to demands for accountability by external funding sources as well as internal users. These demands are often functionally unrelated so that existing data sets do not represent all, if many, of the primary components in an agency system. Therefore, the selection of quantitative methodologies, including modeling, for analyses of these entities can be quite limited. Missing data, however, often can be developed for current activities. In modeling exercises, soft variables based on reasonable assumptions can substitute, if necessary, because the relative behaviors of model components, rather than specific values of statistical parameters, are of equal, if not primary, importance. These assumptions must be as realistic as possible. Analysts and others must realize, however, that the use and results of these methodologies are quite different from those using only numerical data (for example, multiple regression).

Oregon's Experience

In 1993 the Oregon Employment Department (OED) expanded its performance measurement efforts by incorporating various process-improvement techniques, including systems modeling procedures. One component of this program was based on a model put forth by Daniel Kim (1990) that proposed the synthesis of systems modeling and the principles of Total Quality Management (TQM) to facilitate organizational learning. Kim called this model Systemic Quality Management (SQM). According to Kim, TQM serves the operational component well. For the conceptual level, however, Kim (and others) suggests the methodology of systems thinking, which Richmond (1994) defines as "the art and science of making reliable inferences about behavior by developing an increasingly deep understanding of underlying structure."

Further opportunity to use systems modeling as a tool in agency evaluation arose in 1996 when the Joint Legislative Audit Committee requested that the Legislative Fiscal Office (LFO) conduct a program evaluation of the Oregon Commission on Children and Families (OCCF). In addition, the Secretary of State's Audits Division concurrently conducted a performance audit of the OCCF. Of particular interest were the high, initial levels of OCCF administrative costs.

In 1993 House Bill (HB) 2004 had created the OCCF due to concerns regarding possibly fragmented and uncoordinated services to families. The OCCF is a unique organization of county commissions and a central state agency intended to provide preventive, locally integrated services for children and families. HB 2004 empowered counties and county commissions to create and implement comprehensive social service plans that address the particular needs of each locale. This system fundamentally departed from established procedures for centralized state-funded programs. Four key principles are evident in HB 2004: local decision making, "wellness," system integration, and outcome measurement. HB 2004 states that outcome effectiveness would be determined by performance measures linked to the Oregon Benchmarks, a broad array of social, economic, and environmental health indicators. This specific accountability, as indicated by performance measures and linked to the benchmarks, is a natural focus for any evaluation of this system.

Model Development. To provide a conceptual framework for study, we developed, as one study component, a systems model of the state and local organizations using ithink® software. We believed that this approach would enable us to evaluate comprehensive effects of current and potential policy and management decisions on stated and assumed goals of the OCCF. Our ultimate goal was to determine which combinations of agency components increased long-term effectiveness, relative to a base level, and the relative change in the values of those components. We could thus identify the critical parts of the agency business process to target for further analysis and possible future improvements.

For basic data and analyses, we randomly selected twelve of the thirty-six counties as the sampling set. We surveyed local commissions and service providers and conducted visits to each of the twelve counties to interview local commissioners, commission directors, and selected providers. To determine community partners' opinions regarding the commission's overall effectiveness, we surveyed over two hundred local human services organizations, including other state and county agencies. These methodologies yielded a large and comprehensive set of data concerning budgetary and programmatic activities and outcomes.

Using a systems approach for our study seemed appropriate for four reasons:

- It forced us to study, understand, and then duplicate both the functions and functional relationships within the OCCF.
- Modeling the system enabled an understanding of how the primary components interact to affect program outcomes and, it was hoped, clients' qualities of life.
- The great complexity and still-developing nature of this service delivery system precluded a systematic, statistical analysis of data. In fact, the agency lacked consistent data sets for important processes and outcomes.
- We could test various alternatives to the existing management structure to support policy recommendations based on conventional evaluation techniques.

We began the modeling exercise by meeting with OCCF executive staff to ascertain the system's components and their functional relationships. We continually refined our product using all other data-gathering activities, as well as further discussions with agency staff. For example, we developed clarification questions for inclusion into the subsequent local commission and provider questionnaires. Answers to these questions contained process information that could be used to refine the model as well as characterize and investigate important components of the system. Figure 5.1 illustrates the resultant model using ithink® software.

The four high-level sectors denote the primary functions within the system. Stocks, flows, and "converters" represent activities and relationships within the sectors. Stocks accumulate, flows are rates of change, and converters are constants or modifying variables. Some initial values are based on

Figure 5.1. Systems Model of the Oregon Commission on
Children and Families

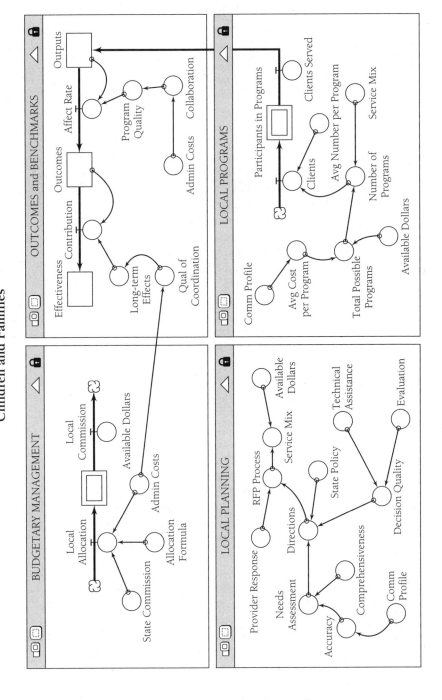

OCCF data; others represent our best assumptions and are so indicated (*).
Bivariate relationships are defined by graphs.

   Budgetary Management. This sector represents legislative and state-level
management of the OCCF system. We have represented the primary budgetary
process by connecting the following components:

State Commission. A "converter" that represents an average biennial allocation
   to one county for 1995–1997 and equals $57,000,000 (thirty-six counties,
   or $1,580,000 per county).
Allocation Formula.* A qualitative variable that can weight, or adjust, the county
   allocation to be more or less than the average. By adjusting this converter, one
   can analyze the systemic effects of policy adjustments to this formula.
Admin Costs. A percentage that represents generic administration dollars sub-
   tracted from the allocation. We assume that these dollars primarily pay for staff;
   the greater the "admin" rate, the more staff are available. Admin Costs can also
   be one-time implementation expenses during the first few years of operation.
Local Allocation. A "rate of flow," or the amount per unit time, of dollars from the
   state to a typical local commission after administrative expenditures; it equals:
   (State Commission) × (Allocation Formula) × (1 – Admin Costs). Therefore,
   this variable equals the amount available to spend for service programs.
Local Commission. A "stock" that accumulates the allocation from the state
   and disperses contracted payments to local providers. Local Commission is
   a special type of stock, called an "oven," that accumulates and holds its contents for a specified length of time (one month).
Available Dollars. A rate that represents the total dollars per unit time that are
   available for service programs.

   Local Planning. This sector represents the comprehensive planning process
that occurs within counties and calculates the number of programs that the
local commission will fund. In reality, this process is complex and occurs over
several months; we have simplified it to illustrate primary planning activities.
Local Planning is totally composed of "converters" to simulate better the variety of program areas that might result from the planning process. This series
of converters acts as a string of algebraic equations that incorporates community types, planning quality, the provider community, management controls,
and state policy to calculate the number of funded programs.

Comm (community) Profile.* Represents the socioeconomic diversity of a community that contributes to the need for a greater variety of programs. Diversity is a function of population and the economic-cultural continuum. A
   larger value of Comm Profile indicates the presence of more subpopulations
   of citizens requiring different types of services for wellness. Larger, urban
   areas should exhibit greater values of Comm Profile than rural communities.
Accuracy.* Indicates the degree to which the community mapping and planning process identified all existing needs in the community. For example,

the presence of several ethnic, racial, and cultural groups across all socio-economic classifications might require a greater degree of accuracy to delineate overall community needs than would a more homogeneous area. We assumed that accuracy decreases with increasing community diversity (Figure 5.2). Thus, in the model, Accuracy is a function of Comm Profile; it decreases in value with increasing community complexity.

Comprehensiveness.* Similar to Accuracy, but focuses on the breadth of the mapping and planning efforts across the total community. Comprehensiveness is a value between 0 and 5; the greater the value is, the more comprehensive the efforts are.

Needs Assessment.* An overall indicator of the quality of the mapping-planning process; equals (Accuracy × Comprehensiveness). This calculation yields a value that is used to represent the potential number of different programs that could be funded by the Local Commission regardless of available funding.

State Policy. Equals eleven, the number of mandatory benchmarks that counties must address in their plans. Some Local Commissions fund at least one program per Benchmark. Therefore, State Policy is the minimum number of programs that a county funds.

Technical Assistance.* Represents positive and corrective input from the state commission and benefits the planning process; its value can vary between 0 and 2.0.

Evaluation.* The effect of beneficial oversight by the state; its value can vary between 0 and 2.0.

Decision Quality.* Indicates the degree of adequacy of the total planning process and a broad quality control function by management; it equals [(Technical Assistance) × (Evaluation)].

Directions. A number that represents the final set of potential programs; its value equals the largest of State Policy or Needs Assessment times Decision Quality. Thus, the concept of quality mitigates the service selection process;

Figure 5.2. Accuracy as a Function of Community Profile

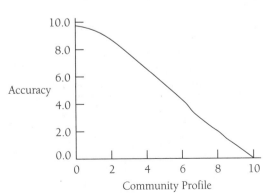

in the long term, it will diminish the number of client outcomes if oversight and judgment are inadequate.

Provider Response.* A value between 0 and 1.0; it represents an assessment of the quality of responses to the county requests for proposals (RFPs) for services; it varies directly with the number and appropriateness of provider responses. It reflects the pool of potential respondents and mitigates the final number of programs.

RFP Process. Equals [(Directions) × (Provider Response)]; it represents a bottleneck in the system if Provider Response is less than maximal because the realized number of funded programs will not equal the potential number.

Service Mix. Equals RFP Process when Available Dollars is more than zero. It represents both qualitative and quantitative aspects of the final set of contracted services.

Available Dollars. A duplicate of the variable in Budgetary Management.

Local Programs. In this sector, we compare the results of the Local Planning sector to the maximum number of potential programs based on the total allocation to the Local Commission. Clients now enter the funded programs en masse at an average and constant rate per program. After admission, clients remain in the program for eighteen months, after which they leave the program as short-term outputs.

Comm Profile. The same here as it is in the Local Planning sector.

Avg (average) Cost per Program.* A function of Comm Profile. We assumed that costly programs would be necessary as community complexity increases (Figure 5.3).

Available Dollars. Like Comm Profile, duplicated in this sector.

Total Possible Programs. Equals [(Available Dollars) × (Avg Cost per Program)]; this is the maximum number that can be funded by a county.

Figure 5.3. Average Cost per Program as a Function of Community Profile

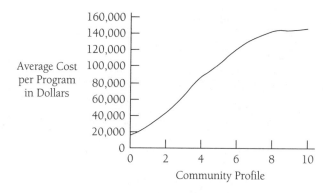

Service Mix. A duplicate from Local Planning.

Number of Programs. The final number of programs available to clients in a county. We wanted to represent a decision point regarding the number of programs that can be directly funded with state dollars versus the number of programs resulting from the planning process. Therefore, Number of Programs can equal Service Mix or Total Possible Programs. We assumed that counties would fund the necessary, but minimal, number of programs. Therefore, if Service Mix and Total Possible Programs differ, which is usually the case, and Service Mix is smaller than Total Possible Programs, then Number of Programs will equal Service Mix. If not, it equals Total Possible Programs.

Avg (average) Number per Program. The average number of participants per program. It can vary between 10 and 500; we held it constant at 85.

Clients. The total number of citizens who enter the programs.

Participants in Programs. Another stock wherein clients stay for eighteen months, the period of time in which clients participate in programs. For simplicity, no one drops out and all participants finish their programs.

Clients Served. The number of participants leaving the programs after receiving services.

Outcomes and Benchmarks. This sector of the model converts program outputs into units of effectiveness, otherwise known as Benchmarks. It is the most idealized and theoretical portion of the system because these relationships are the most dubious and least substantiated. Various agency components and characteristics affect this transformation in a participant's quality of life.

Outputs. Simple counts of the program participants; Outputs equal Clients Served.

Admin Costs. A duplicate.

Collaboration.* Represents the holistic benefit of interagency activities. In this case, Collaboration is a function of Admin Costs and ranges in value from 0 to 1.0 (Figure 5.4).

Program Quality.* Represents how well the programs, overall, perform their functions, or their effectiveness. Program Quality is a function of Collaboration (Figure 5.5).

Affect Rate. The rate of change from outputs to outcomes; a mathematical representation of the positive change in a client's life. We assume that interagency collaboration and the quality of the program combine to produce a potentially significant change.

Outcomes. The numbers of outputs that experience a true benefit from their respective programs.

Qual (quality) of Coordination.* Represents coordination activities by local commission staff among county and state agencies and others. Qual of Coordination is a function of Admin Costs (Figure 5.6); we assume that the benefits of coordinating activities generally increase with increasing staff time and then reach a plateau. This variable differs from Collaboration because it

Figure 5.4. Collaboration as a Function of Administrative Costs

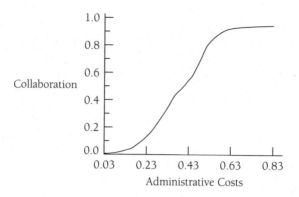

Figure 5.5. Program Quality as a Function of Collaboration

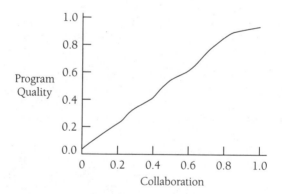

Figure 5.6. Quality of Coordination as a Function of Administrative Costs

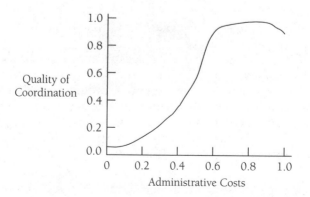

incorporates operations focused on long-range goals; Collaboration is more focused on short-term adjustments to specific programs.

Long-term Effects.* Represents those long-lasting changes in clients' lives achieved by successful programs. We assume that Long-term Effects will increase with increasing quality of coordination (Figure 5.7).

Contribution. The rate of change from program outcomes to units of true Effectiveness.

Effectiveness. Represents the Oregon Benchmarks. Refers to counts of individuals exhibiting some benefit of their respective programs.

Validation of the Model. Due to the agency's lack of comprehensive outcome data, we could not compare specific levels of key output variables, such as Outcomes and Long-term Effects, with existing agency results to verify the model's effectiveness absolutely. During the model-building phase, however, we did incorporate OCCF management data into the model's equations wherever possible. Iterative discussions with OCCF staff indicated that the subsequent behaviors of the model components were appropriate. We therefore assumed that the overall behavior of the model was valid.

Results of the Model. When confronted by critics, proponents of OCCF's decentralized, community-based system defend the agency's high level of administrative costs as necessary and short-term expenditures during its implementation phase. In response to this potential policy issue, we focused our analysis on the systemwide effects of varying rates of administrative overhead. Specifically we assumed that increased administrative expenditures result in increasing levels of staff or full-time equivalents. We used the sensitivity mode of the software to repeat all calculations as it varies the value of one variable based on a predetermined range.

We first varied Admin Costs from 0.03 to 0.85 over ten iterations to establish a baseline. Thus, we designated from 3 percent to 85 percent of a county's total biennial allocation to centralized staff, thereby decreasing the

**Figure 5.7 Long-Term Effects as a Function of Quality
and Coordination**

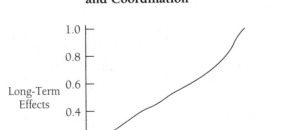

corresponding dollars available for service programs. Then we performed four sets of these same ten iterations as follows:

1. Long-term Effects and Program Quality both equal 1.0; the equations are not functioning. This condition represents an idealized future management scenario whereby the service programs operate as effectively as possible.
2. Long-term Effects equals 1.0, and Program Quality is determined by its equation.
3. Condition 2 is reversed.
4. Both equations are functioning.

By comparing the resulting values of Effectiveness after twenty-four months, we could evaluate a rather limited set of potential scenarios. Figure 5.8 illustrates the results of these runs. Under the conditions of the first scenario, all clients exit the programs as "changed" individuals; these services impart significant and positive benefits to them. Thus, the number of clients entering and exiting the programs equals the value of Effectiveness for each value of Admin Costs. The perfect combination of staffing level and functionality of centralized management is in place. In this case, the primary effect of increasing administrative expenditures is a decreasing number of programs with a corresponding decrease in the number of exiting clients.

When Program Quality is a function of Collaboration and, ultimately, Admin Costs, and Long-term Effects is constant and maximal (scenario 2), clients benefit when increasing levels of centralized staff efficiently coordinate programs. Maximal benefits require greater investments in effective staff. The

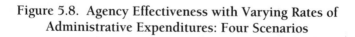

Figure 5.8. Agency Effectiveness with Varying Rates of Administrative Expenditures: Four Scenarios

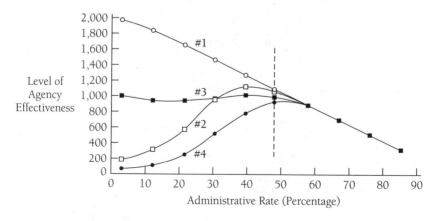

county must invest almost 40 percent of the total allocation in management staff to realize 57 percent (1,121 ÷ 1,976) of its potential effectiveness.

In scenario 3, Program Quality is constant and maximal, and Long-term Effects is a function of Qual of Coordination and, ultimately, Admin Costs. In this case, the initial level of effectiveness is almost six times that for the previous alternative (998 versus 173). In addition, these levels remain fairly constant until the overriding consequence of decreasing dollars for programs reduces them. Evidently management efforts that focus on maximizing program effectiveness shortly after completion are of greater value than investing in staffing levels for longer-term planning. When Admin Costs is approximately 40 percent, however, the effectiveness level of scenario 2 is slightly greater than this one, probably due to the decreased number of total clients who are enrolling in fewer programs.

Overall program effectiveness is minimal when both Program Quality and Long-term Effects are functions of other variables (scenario 4). The values of program effectiveness are the least of any of the four scenarios, although the number of clients entering and exiting the programs remains the same. The combined effects of lower levels of program management evidently result in this minimal productivity.

In general, the dominant systems effect is that of decreasing funds for service programs associated with increasing management effectiveness. Under the assumptions of the model, low administrative rates result in management staffing levels that are not sufficient to produce effective programs. When sufficient staffing is realized, reductions in program allocations (due to higher staffing costs) limit overall effectiveness. If additional research upheld our basic assumption that management effectiveness increases with increasing investment, then the agency could justify administrative rates as high as 50 percent, the optimal level for this situation.

We assumed that both increasing numbers and resulting efficiency levels of agency and local staff for coordination, collaboration, and general program management activities contribute to the overall long-term effectiveness of the OCCF system. The model indicated that there is an optimal level for investing in staff for these activities. If the basic objective is to increase long-term effectiveness (measured by Benchmark values), then a trade-off occurs between funding services to maximize program "outputs" and paying for efforts by staff to develop service integration. When staff activities are below this optimal level, then long-term effectiveness declines due to insignificant collaboration. However, when activities exceed this level, insufficient funds go to local services, and program outcomes decline.

OCCF staff believe that comprehensive and accurate planning is important in determining both the number of programs and the long-term effectiveness of the process. We did not connect components of Local Planning into Outcomes and Benchmarks in this version of the model. As a next step in an ongoing process, analysts could establish specific links between these sectors to refine the model.

Conclusion

Several conclusions emerge from our modeling exercise. The first is that the lack of agency data limited our ability to validate the model fully. Although we included actual rates and numbers when possible, we were uncomfortable with the number of assumptions that we had to make, especially concerning management components and program effectiveness. For example, the OCCF could not quantify overall the effectiveness of its local programs. These gaps represent needs that should be rectified and, as such, comprise the basis for several recommendations in our report. Based on discussions with agency staff, we believe that these assumptions were appropriate and reasonable so that the modeling exercise was a valuable part of the overall evaluation. Thus, modeling cannot substitute for missing data but can significantly contribute to an effective study.

Appropriate data for actually testing the effectiveness of the OCCF system may never exist. Although integrated, multiagency databases do exist in Oregon, the high resource demands of building adequate systems on a statewide scale, compared to the currently lowered political priority of the potential OCCF information, probably preclude future investments in comprehensive data development. Therefore, staff need to research and implement accurate qualitative methodologies to provide appropriate information, especially regarding management effectiveness, to continue evaluation programs, including modeling exercises.

Given these drawbacks, we nevertheless believe that the modeling exercise was quite valuable. By defining and linking the components of this system, we gained an understanding of the theoretical and actual processes and organizations of the OCCF. However, we could have acquired additional data and information for specific linkages and components of the model with an additional and large investment of time and resources that was beyond the scope of the original study.

Analysts probably would not discover the overall system behavior illustrated in Figure 5.8 using independent, conventional analyses. For example, the Secretary of State Audits Division simultaneously conducted a routine program audit "in accordance with generally accepted government auditing standards" (Oregon Secretary of State Audits Division 1996). The auditors focused on the OCCF's administration expenditures and determined that the overall administrative rate was 42 percent; $42 of each $100 of expenditures paid for administration, and $58 paid for direct services to clients. They recommended a 10 percent rate for local commissions and service providers with estimated savings of $1.2 to $1.5 million per biennium.

From the unilateral viewpoint of an auditor, this recommendation is proper. When considering the systemwide effects of changing administrative rates, however, we would not be so definitive. Indeed we concluded that greater administrative expenditures (40 to 50 percent) during the OCCF's implementation phase might be appropriate. These two views typify current differences between classical foci of auditing and general program evaluation (Brooks, 1996).

Systems modeling can be a useful tool in evaluations for legislators. Because legislation often affects multiple agencies or issues, models based on budgetary, staffing, and process relationships can provide relevant insights for policy recommendations. Indeed, Marvin (1979) states that program evaluation can be "a function intended to assist future policy and management decisions." To this end, systems modeling can provide more comprehensive, if not more functionally accurate, indications and answers for the legislative process.

Evaluating offices, however, must allocate adequate time and staff to perform an initial, comprehensive assessment of data availability, as well as a complete modeling exercise. Therefore staff should make a prudent assessment of the probability for completion of this exercise given the time, resources, and data available to them.

When communicating aspects of the modeling exercise, evaluators should be cognizant of a potential negative reaction to this topic. Of course, reactions vary with individual readers. Many individuals, including legislators, however, would be reluctant to attempt an understanding of systems modeling because they might consider this methodology too theoretical, too complex, and too academic. Although we did not specifically refer to the modeling exercise during our oral presentation to the committee, we did include appropriate conclusions that resulted from this methodology, as well as a chapter on the modeling exercise in the written report. Using common terms instead of technical jargon facilitates communication between staff and legislators.

In summary, we found that systems modeling was a valuable part of our evaluation. Although the OCCF lacked outcome data for use in validating our model, we gained several unique insights into the overall management of this agency. We then incorporated this knowledge into our report to the legislature.

References

Brooks, R. A. "Blending Two Cultures: State Legislative Auditing and Evaluation." In C. Wisler (ed.), *Evaluation and Auditing: Prospects for Convergence.* New Directions for Evaluation, no. 71. San Francisco: Jossey-Bass, 1996.

Cochrane, D. D., Kestle, J., Steinbok, P., Evans, D., and Heron, N. "Model for the Cost Analysis of Shunted Hydrocephalic Children." *Pediatric Neurosurgery,* 1995, *23,* 14–19.

Kim, D. H. "Toward Learning Organizations: Integrating Total Quality Control and Systems Thinking." Unpublished paper, 1990.

Marvin, K. E. "Evaluation for Congressional Committees: The Quest for Effective Procedures." In F. M. Zweig (ed.), *Evaluation in Legislation.* Sage Research Progress Series in Evaluation, vol. 5. Thousand Oaks, Calif.: Sage, 1979.

Morecroft, J.D.W. "System Dynamics and Microworlds for Policymakers." *European Journal of Operational Research,* 1988, *35,* 301–320.

Oregon Secretary of State Audits Division. *Oregon Commission on Children and Families: Funding and Use of Local Services.* Report No. 96–54. Nov. 20, 1996.

Richmond, B. "Systems Dynamics/Systems Thinking—Let's Just Get On with It." Paper presented at the International System Dynamics Conference, Sterling, Scotland, 1994.

Stokey, E., and Zeckhauser, R. *A Primer for Policy Analysis.* New York: Norton, 1978.

Weiss, C. H. "Introduction." In C. H. Weiss (ed.), *Using Social Research in Public Policy-Making.* Lexington, Mass.: Heath, 1977.

PATRICK W. MCINTIRE *is policy, performance, and program analyst with the Oregon Employment Department. Previously he was legislative analyst with the Oregon Legislative Fiscal Office.*

ANN S. GLAZE *is senior legislative analyst with the Oregon Legislative Fiscal Office.*

The use of convergent policy analysis approaches enables legislative program evaluators to assess questions that are not framed with research feasibility in mind.

Convergent Policy Analysis

Desmond Saunders-Newton, Gregory J. Rest, Wayne M. Turnage

In the face of a national movement for environmental justice, the Virginia General Assembly directed its legislative oversight agency in 1993 to study practices related to the siting, monitoring, and cleanup of solid waste facilities, specifically focusing on the impact of these activities on minority communities. The key issue raised by the assembly's mandate was whether a pattern of racial discrimination had developed in the process for siting and monitoring solid waste management facilities that disproportionately exposes minorities to certain health risks. Although the study found no evidence of an intent to discriminate against minorities, the analysis revealed that in some cases, siting and monitoring practices have had a disproportionate impact on minority communities.

The report resulting from this legislative mandate includes a number of significant findings related to the impact of solid waste management facilities on minority communities. Here we focus less on presenting these issues than on describing the structured use of multiple and disparate analytical techniques to develop a cogent and clarifying representation of these issues to a legislative body concerned with making appropriate choices in the future. We view the formal and focused use of quantitative and qualitative techniques from various disciplines as convergent policy analysis. This approach to analysis emphasizes the importance of designing policy studies and program evaluations in a fashion that allows for using results from disparate techniques such that they converge on similar policy solutions. This approach allows for the generation of preponderant evidence in support of a particular social outcome or policy recommendation.

Overview of Solid Waste Siting Study

In 1993 the Virginia General Assembly passed House Joint Resolution 529 directing the Joint Legislative Audit and Review Commission (JLARC) to study practices related to solid waste facilities, specifically focusing on the impact of these activities on minority communities. The concerns expressed in this study mandate mirror those articulated nationwide by a growing number of community action groups. Convinced that minorities face greater exposure to environmental pollutants, these groups are pressuring federal, state, and local officials to reform a siting process that they contend deliberately targets minority communities as potential sites for solid waste management facilities.

The Environmental Justice Movement in Virginia. The issue of whether race is a key factor in the siting of solid waste management facilities had its roots more than ten years ago when a landfill was constructed in a predominantly black North Carolina county and specifically to receive the highly toxic chemical PCB. Following a nationally publicized protest of this siting, several studies were conducted that concluded that hazardous waste facilities were more likely to be located in areas with high proportions of minority residents.

In response to the growing pressure from members of what is now referred to as the environmental justice movement, the U.S. Environmental Protection Agency (EPA) formed a task force in 1993 to examine the issue. In 1994 President Clinton signed an executive order directing the relevant federal agencies to take immediate action regarding the issue of environmental justice.

Prior to House Joint Resolution 529, there had been no systematic study of this issue in Virginia. However, the decision to locate several landfills and a medical waste incinerator in localities with large minority populations produced a controversial impetus for the legislative mandate that led to the original study.

The perception held by members of the environmental justice movement suggested that although the patterns observed in Virginia had not been rigorously examined, they were consistent with national data that clearly indicated that race played a role in the decision-making process for the siting of solid waste facilities. Based largely on this anecdotal evidence, some members of this movement argued strongly for reforming the process for siting facilities in the Commonwealth of Virginia.

Study Approach. The approach used in the *Solid Waste Facility Management in Virginia: Impact on Minority Communities* report was designed to assess directly whether locality siting practices for solid waste management facilities may be racially based, thereby imposing a disproportionate share of the potential environmental hazards associated with the operation of these facilities on minority communities. The study mandate recognized that if minorities are more likely to live close to solid waste management facilities (SWMFs), any inadequacies in the procedures used to inspect and monitor these facilities could increase their risk of exposure to environmental pollutants should problems develop at these sites.

As a result, the framework developed by JLARC staff for this review was designed to examine how the practices related to solid waste facility siting, monitoring, and cleanup are conducted and whether there is evidence to indicate that minorities are likely to bear a disproportionate burden of any problems associated with the oversight areas of solid waste management in Virginia. JLARC staff sought to develop a study approach that would address environmental equity questions such as these:

- Are waste facilities located in communities with disproportionately minority populations?
- Is there evidence of a specific intent to locate the facilities in minority communities?
- Is there a difference in the level of state oversight and inspection between facilities in minority and white communities?

Examining State and Local Siting Policies and Practices. JLARC staff conducted a number of research activities to address the environmental equity research questions. With respect to the first two questions, the central issue of the study mandate was to determine whether minority communities are being targeted when decisions are made concerning where SWMFs will be located. To support this issue, the staff had to conduct two major activities: (1) identify the racial composition of the communities in which SWMFs have been sited since the passage of the solid waste regulations in 1988, and (2) conduct structured interviews with officials and stakeholders at both the state and local levels who were involved in the siting process. These efforts allowed for defining the communities or neighborhoods in which solid waste facilities have been located and to evaluate, in part, whether there were racial differences associated with the sitings.

In order to complete the siting analysis, JLARC staff had to determine what constituted a solid waste community and identify the racial composition of this community. Based on previous studies and interviews with state and local officials, JLARC staff defined the community as the area that includes census blocks within a two-mile radius surrounding the SWMF.

Next, using data on the longitude and latitude of all facilities that have been granted permits to operate since 1988, JLARC staff pinpointed these sites on a 1990 census database and used a geographical mapping system to draw a two-mile radius around each site as a means of defining the solid waste community. This database organizes information on Virginia's population at the block, block group, and census tract levels. The block is the smallest unit of analysis in the census data and for confidentiality reasons contains less information than the larger block groups and census tracts. Block groups are predetermined clusters of the individual blocks, and the census tracts represent an aggregation of the block groups at the county and city levels.

With mapping software, JLARC staff were able to work with the smallest unit of analysis and identify those blocks whose geographical midpoint fell within the two-mile radius used to define the landfill community. Using data on the race of the residents from these blocks, the proportion of minorities in the communities was calculated and compared to the racial composition for the locality in which the community was located.

The statistical analysis indicates whether the communities in which solid waste facilities are sited are in predominantly minority neighborhoods or whether these areas have a disproportionate number of minorities. The limitation is that it does not explain the cause of these outcomes. In other words, it does not indicate whether this impact reflects an intentional bias in the siting process or is due to other factors that appear to be related to the racial composition of the communities in which facilities are sited.

To examine this question, JLARC staff conducted structured interviews with local community groups, the county or city administrators, members of the local boards of supervisors and city councils, and the facilities managers in the localities in which the SWMFs were sited. The respondents were asked to recreate the siting process and provide documentation supporting their descriptions. With this information, the team could determine if key differences existed in the siting process for localities according to the racial composition of the solid waste communities.

Another focus of this study was to determine how much the residents knew about the siting process. Since 1988 more than thirty SWMFs have been granted permits to receive solid waste. The data that JLARC staff used in this assessment were collected using a telephone survey of a sample of residents from each solid waste community established since 1988. Through a contract with the Virginia Commonwealth University (VCU) Survey Research Laboratory, JLARC staff were able to determine whether residents living near SWMFs had any knowledge about the siting process. To conduct the survey, VCU identified a random sample of households in each solid waste community established since 1988 and conducted a telephone survey in which the residents were asked a series of questions about the SWMF in their area.

Assessment of Department of Environmental Quality Monitoring and Enforcement Practices. The study design also emphasized the assessment of the Virginia Department of Environmental Quality's (DEQ) monitoring and enforcement practices. This portion of the analysis was viewed as important since legislative actions in 1988 designed to strengthen solid waste regulations increased DEQ's responsibilities substantially. These oversight responsibilities included required regular inspections of solid waste facilities, the implementation of enforcement actions against noncompliant facilities, and the inspection of facilities that stopped receiving waste to determine if they were properly closed. To evaluate the adequacy of DEQ's oversight efforts, JLARC staff reviewed the agency's records detailing their inspection, enforcement, and closed-site monitoring activities.

For each oversight function, JLARC staff analyzed whether the agency's activities were implemented without regard to the race of the community surrounding the SWMFs. As with the analysis of siting, JLARC used 1990 census block data with the mapping software package to identify the racial composition of the communities surrounding the sites examined in the analysis. Structured interviews were also conducted with DEQ inspectors and enforcement staff to supplement the analysis of the files.

Methodological Preponderance

The JLARC study approach emphasized the use of multiple approaches. The use of multiple research methods allows for the generation of insights that are more rigorous when the storyline resulting from each analysis converges in the same direction, in support of the same research thesis. This use of multiple research perspectives follows from what is defined in qualitative methods literature as triangulation analysis (Patton, 1987). It is used whenever possible in research at JLARC, given time and resource constraints. Here we look at convergence analysis and how it was used to structure the analysis of Virginia's SWMF siting and inspection process.

Convergent Policy Analysis. Convergent policy analysis can be defined as the intentional and disciplined use of multiple, and possibly disparate, data sources, research methods, or theoretical perspectives to examine a policy issue or evaluate a program. This approach emphasizes the importance of designing policy studies and program evaluations in a fashion that allows for using results from disparate techniques such that they "converge" on similar policy insights and solutions. This approach can result in both an improved grasp of the strengths and weaknesses of the study, as well as the techniques used in the study, and the generation of preponderant evidence in support of a given social outcome or policy recommendation.

This approach is based on triangulation, which assumes, given that any one data collection or inquiry strategy has both strengths and weaknesses, that using more than one collection or inquiry approach permits the analyst or evaluator to combine strengths and correct some of the deficiencies of any one source of data.

Convergence and Solid Waste Management Facility Siting Analysis. Although the study found no evidence of an intent to discriminate against minorities, the analysis revealed that in some cases, siting and monitoring practices have had a disproportionate impact on minority communities.

Minorities are disproportionately affected by 35 percent of SWMF sitings. JLARC's analysis of the racial composition of the communities surrounding the recently sited SWMFs reveal that approximately seven of every ten residents who live within communities around newly permitted SWMFs are white. In addition, only seven of forty-one communities (17 percent) around these sites have a minority population that exceeded 50 percent (Figure 6.1).

Nonetheless, legitimate questions can be raised about facility sitings patterns showing that minorities live near SWMFs at rates that are higher than should be expected based on their numbers in the overall population of the locality. This type of disproportionate representation suggests that minorities

Figure 6.1. Racial Characteristics of Neighborhoods with Solid Waste Sites

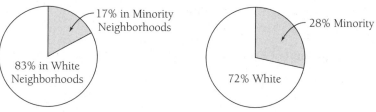

17% in Minority Neighborhoods

83% in White Neighborhoods

Proportions of Sites That Are in Minority Versus White Neighborhoods

28% Minority

72% White

Aggregate Racial Composition of All Site Neighborhoods

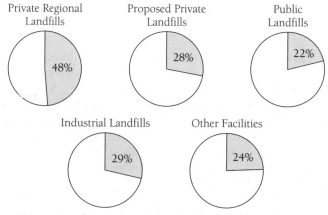

Private Regional Landfills

48%

Proposed Private Landfills

28%

Public Landfills

22%

Industrial Landfills

29%

Other Facilities

24%

Proportion of Minorities in the Neighborhoods Surrounding Recently Permitted Sites or Proposed Landfills, by Facility Type

Note: In this study, minority neighborhood is defined as a neighborhood where more than 50 percent of the residents are minorities.

Source: JLARC staff analysis of 1990 census block data and information from the Virginia Department of Environmental Quality.

are, either coincidentally or as a matter of public policy, subject to a disproportionate share of any burdens or risks that may be associated with living in close proximity to an SWMF.

The study findings suggest that minorities are disproportionately affected by 35 percent of the SWMF sitings (Figure 6.2). Fourteen of the forty (35 percent) planned or established facilities since 1988 are in communities that are disproportionately minority. In seven of these fourteen facility sitings that are considered to have a disproportionate impact, the differences between the community and the locality-wide minority rate are greater than 20 percentage points.

Figure 6.2. Impact of Solid Waste Facility Sitings on Minority Communities

Proportion of Sites in Disproportionately* Minority Communities

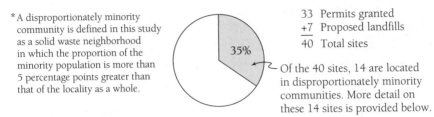

* A disproportionately minority community is defined in this study as a solid waste neighborhood in which the proportion of the minority population is more than 5 percentage points greater than that of the locality as a whole.

35%

33 Permits granted
+7 Proposed landfills
40 Total sites

Of the 40 sites, 14 are located in disproportionately minority communities. More detail on these 14 sites is provided below.

Minority Population Rates of Solid Waste Neighborhoods Compared to the Localities' Overall Minority Rates

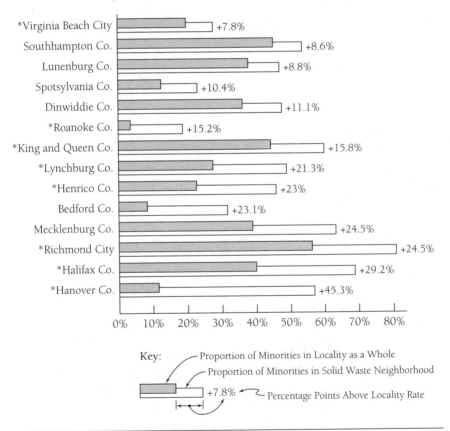

*Virginia Beach City +7.8%
Southhampton Co. +8.6%
Lunenburg Co. +8.8%
Spotsylvania Co. +10.4%
Dinwiddie Co. +11.1%
*Roanoke Co. +15.2%
*King and Queen Co. +15.8%
*Lynchburg Co. +21.3%
*Henrico Co. +23%
Bedford Co. +23.1%
Mecklenburg Co. +24.5%
*Richmond City +24.5%
*Halifax Co. +29.2%
*Hanover Co. +45.3%

0%   10%   20%   30%   40%   50%   60%   70%   80%

Key: ⌐ Proportion of Minorities in Locality as a Whole
      ⌐ Proportion of Minorities in Solid Waste Neighborhood
      +7.8% ⌐ Percentage Points Above Locality Rate

---

*In these localities, the neighborhood surrounding the site includes residents from adjacent jurisdictions.

Source: JLARC staff analysis of data from the Virginia Department of Environmental Quality and 1990 census blocks.

There is no evidence of intent to target minority communities. Despite the disproportionate impact on minorities, there is no evidence of an intent to discriminate against these communities. A review of the local decision-making process in these and other communities did not reveal significant differences between the siting process for sites in disproportionately minority communities. Localities that approved solid waste sites in minority communities were just as likely to have conducted formal independent siting studies and objectively evaluated alternative sites and were almost as likely to have had minority representatives on the local governing board who supported the siting decision.

Public participation in the process needs to be improved. One aspect of the siting process that needs to be improved is public participation. In a number of localities JLARC visited, the lack of public involvement during the early stages of the siting process was apparent. In some of the more urban localities, much of the planning for the site was handled by professional staff and consultants. In some of the more rural localities, county administrators and members of the board of supervisors worked closely on the project without much outside involvement.

A survey of residents in communities with SWMFs that have been permitted under the 1988 regulations indicates that public participation in the siting process generally has not been cultivated. Only 15 percent of those responding to the survey had any knowledge of how the facility came to be located in their community, and 77 percent indicated that they had no knowledge about the siting of the facility in their community. The number of minority residents with any knowledge of the siting process was even lower: only 8 percent. In minority communities, failure to involve the public in a meaningful way during the early stages of the process may give rise to suspicion and resentment that the site is being "dumped" in the community because of the racial composition of the residents.

DEQ's inspection process is inconsistent and varies by race. Examination of DEQ's inspection process over the past twenty-three years revealed significant problems with the process that are at least partly the result of the chronic staff shortages among inspectors and a lack of guidance from the department's central office. The analysis revealed the inspectors are not able to conduct inspections consistently of SWMFs in their region. Further, the length of time between inspections is considerable and especially long for sites in minority neighborhoods (Figure 6.3). Also, the length of time that sites remain out of compliance with solid waste regulations has increased over time, and the periods of noncompliance have been especially lengthy for sites in minority communities (Figure 6.4).

Solid waste operators that do not resolve violations are referred to the agency's enforcement unit. Data analyzed for the Solid Waste Facility Management Study indicate that the process is underutilized, protracted, and weak. From 1980 to the time of the review only 148 cases had been officially referred to the unit. Most were still pending after an average of three years since the initial referral. Because DEQ does not have the authority to levy administrative penalties without the consent of the operator, some cases are referred to the attorney general's office for legal action. These cases remained unresolved after an average of six years.

Figure 6.3. Time Between Inspections, by Time Period and Community Racial Composition

Time Period One: 1971–1983

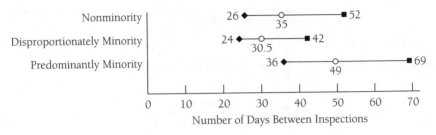

Number of Days Between Inspections

Time Period Two: 1984–1988

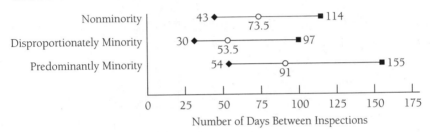

Number of Days Between Inspections

Time Period Three: 1989–1994

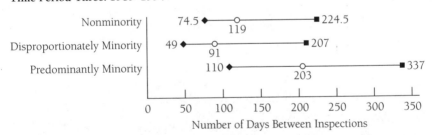

Number of Days Between Inspections

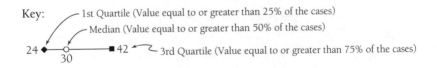

Key: ─ 1st Quartile (Value equal to or greater than 25% of the cases)
      ─ Median (Value equal to or greater than 50% of the cases)
      ─ 3rd Quartile (Value equal to or greater than 75% of the cases)

Source: Department of Environmental Quality data and 1990 census block data.

Figure 6.4. Time to Compliance, by Time Period and Community Racial Composition

Time Period One: 1971–1983

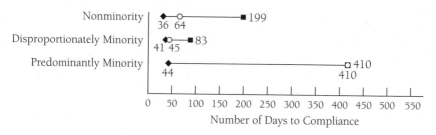

Time Period Two: 1984–1988

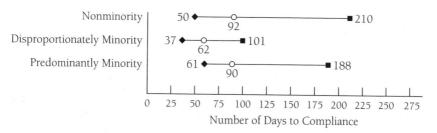

Time Period Three: 1989–1994

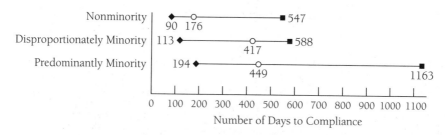

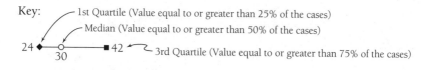

Source: Department of Environmental Quality data and 1990 census block data.

Role of Convergent Policy Analysis. These findings, among others, which are the products of a convergent policy analysis approach, resulted in a number of recommendations for future legislative and executive branch action and have been followed by an explicit study of the DEQ's organizational structure and management. The use of statistical and analytical mapping or geographic database techniques allowed assessing the issue of minority disproportionality. Qualitative techniques such as structured interviews, file reviews, and telephone surveys provided a means of examining whether an intent to discriminate existed and the current level of public participation. In addition, the explicit combination of analytical mapping and file reviews helped the JLARC staff to ascertain the inconsistent inspection process of Virginia's DEQ.

These findings would not have been possible by using statistical and analytical mapping alone or survey research and qualitative methods alone. A useful contrast is with a 1995 *Journal of Policy Analysis and Management* article, "Testing for Environmental Racism: Prejudice, Profits, Political Power?" by James Hamilton. In this analysis, Hamilton looks at a number of hypotheses concerned with why exposure to environmental risks may vary by race and suggests that the best explanation for differences in the exposure to risk, given a focus on capacity decisions by commercial hazardous waste facilities, is associated with the differences in the probability that residents will raise a firm's expected location costs by engaging in collective action to oppose capacity siting.

This work and its underlying methods are more than acceptable and consistent with some of the insights garnered from the convergent policy analysis study design, but it would not have generated the findings that ultimately resulted from this JLARC study. More to point, the use of statistics-based methods alone would have led to just one conclusion; the findings from the other information-gathering activities indicated that this one result was only part of the total picture. The fundamental problem was that all persons living near solid waste sites appear to be at risk because inspections are insufficient and that many of these persons are minorities, even though there is no evidence that these persons were targeted because they are minorities. Thus, although determining that siting varies by race is important, it is probably not as big a problem (which was the consensus of legislators on JLARC) as inconsistent monitoring and inspection, which can have an undetected and differential impact on minority communities. Concentrating on just siting would have yielded results that supported policies or legislation specifically aimed at siting problems but missed an issue of much larger scope and relevance in terms of adverse impacts.

Conclusion

JLARC attempts to exploit the advantages of the convergent policy analysis approach whenever possible. The ability to research findings grounded in a variety of perspectives and theories provides measurable benefits in terms of believability and rigor. And it has particularly important and useful aspects for researchers who are conducting legislative program evaluation. This is due to the dual need for analytical capabilities in the legislative branch of Virginia government to ensure the fulfillment of legislative intent and objectives and the political nature of legislative research. Thus, through analytical rigor and the generation of legislative coins for elected officials, the approach effectively supports the two masters of legislative program evaluators and policy analyst: the legislature and adherence to a disciplined inquiry paradigm.

The use of the convergent policy analysis approach requires the commitment of legislatures for strong analytical products and staff willingness to develop a strong repertoire of quantitative and qualitative expertise in assessing legislative issues and programs. This ability will become more important as funding and programs are devolved from the federal level and placed in the purview of states.

References

Hamilton, J. "Testing for Environmental Racism: Prejudice, Profits, Political Power?" *Journal of Policy Analysis and Management,* 1995, *14* (1).

Patton, M. Q. *How to Use Qualitative Methods in Evaluation.* Thousand Oaks, Calif.: Sage, 1987.

Additional Resources

Anderson, D. L., and others. "Hazardous Waste Facilities: 'Environmental Equity' Issues in Metropolitan Areas." *Evaluation Review,* 1994, *18* (2), 123–140.

Bullard, R. D. *Dumping in Dixie.* Boulder, Colo.: Westview Press, 1990.

Commission for Racial Justice. *Toxic Waste and Race in the United States: A National Report on the Racial and Socio-Economic Characteristics of Communities with Hazardous Waste Sites.* New York: United Church of Christ, 1987.

General Accounting Office (GAO). *Siting of Hazardous Waste Facilities Landfills and Their Correlation with Racial and Economic Status of Surrounding Communities.* Washington, D.C.: U.S. Government Printing Office, 1983.

Guba, E. G., and Lincoln, Y. S. "Epistemological and Methodological Bases of Naturalistic Inquiry." *Educational Communications and Technology Journal,* 1992, *4* (30).

Joint Legislative Audit and Review Commission. *Solid Waste Facility Management in Virginia: Impact on Minority Communities.* Richmond, Va: Commonwealth of Virginia, Jan. 1995.

Mohai, P., and Bryant, B. "Environmental Racism: Reviewing the Evidence." In P. Mohai and B. Bryant (eds.), *Race and the Incidence of Environmental Hazards.* Boulder, Colo.: Westview Press, 1992.

DESMOND SAUNDERS-NEWTON *is the strategic planning and policy analyst for the California State University system office and an adjunct faculty member of the University of Southern California's School of Policy, Planning and Development.*

GREGORY J. REST *is chief methodologist with Virginia's Joint Legislative Audit and Review Commission.*

WAYNE M. TURNAGE *is chief legislative analyst with Virginia's Joint Legislative Audit and Review Commission.*

The Florida Government Accountability Report, an Internet encyclopedia that will change the way evaluation information is delivered, addresses a primary challenge facing legislators and other decision makers: obtaining comprehensive, current, user-friendly information on the performance of state government programs.

How Information Technology Changes Delivery of Evaluation: The Florida Government Accountability Report

Gena C. Wade

Information about what Florida's state government does and how effectively it meets the needs of Florida's citizens is fragmented across many sources. The presentation of this information makes it difficult to compare programs that have similar purposes or activities. To address this problem, the Florida Legislature's Office of Program Policy Analysis and Government Accountability (OPPAGA) created the Florida Government Accountability Report (FGAR), an Internet encyclopedia of Florida's state government that offers descriptive, evaluative, and performance information about state government in one accessible place to benefit the legislature and the public.

FGAR makes an essential contribution to the policymaking debate by providing descriptive information about government activities and performance. FGAR also increases prospects for use of evaluation data because its electronic format and design present manageable amounts of information in a usable form. Finally, FGAR's increasing and future value is apparent as collected performance data and summary evaluation approaches grow more important to legislative decision makers.

Background of Project

OPPAGA was created in 1994 to address legislative information needs and provide evaluation information in new forms. In March 1996 OPPAGA began

The views expressed in this chapter are the author's and should not be construed as representing those of the Florida Office of Program Policy Analysis and Government Accountability.

the FGAR project to provide the legislature with a web-available encyclopedia of descriptive and evaluative information.

Legislative Information Needs. As the legislative entity primarily responsible for evaluating state programs in Florida, OPPAGA works to meet policymakers' needs for evaluation information. Because of their broad policy-setting responsibilities, legislators need information on the range of state government programs and activities. They need easily accessible and summarized information that will allow reasonably quick understanding of programs' responsibilities, funding, and results. They need a research source that allows cross-program tracing of services to client groups and discovery of duplicative responsibilities. In addition legislators and their staff need to be able to communicate this information to constituents.

Florida legislators also have a specific need for performance information and an assessment of the information's quality. As a result of the 1994 Government Performance and Accountability Act, state government is undergoing performance-based program budgeting reform. By statute agencies provide performance measures with their budget request for acceptance or revision by the legislature. OPPAGA advises the legislature on the quality of these performance measures. A final set of measures is adopted in the Appropriations Act, and agencies agree to meet legislatively required performance standards on these measures in the coming year. Exhibit 7.1 shows an example of measures established in the 1998–1999 General Appropriations Act for the Department of Children and Families to manage a program for people with developmental disabilities, with the corresponding performance standards that the legislature requires in fiscal year 1998–1999.

Section 216.163(4), Florida Statutes, authorizes the legislature to award incentives or impose disincentives based on actual performance against standards. Although such actions have not yet been taken, reliable information is essential as a basis for making funding decisions based on state program performance. Legislators need a professional opinion on the quality of the performance measures and the performance data that state agencies provide.

OPPAGA has typically offered evaluation information through publishing performance audits and policy analyses, conducting legislative staff briefings, and making presentations to legislative committees. These are useful products, but they are subject to the static quality of time-limited presentation or paper publication.

FGAR Approach to Information. The FGAR is a tool to answer legislative information needs electronically. It is a World Wide Web site consisting of almost four hundred separate articles, called profiles, of individual state government programs. The profiles, the frame for delivering descriptive and evaluative information on every state program, contain the following elements:

- Program description. Describes why Florida provides the program, how the program operates, and whom it serves. All profiles have hyperlinks to the

Exhibit 7.1. Sample Performance Measure Required Under Performance-Based Program Budgeting

People with Developmental Disabilities:

People in the Community

(Note: The Appropriations Act specifies that the people with Developmental Disabilities Program *"will meet the following standards as required by the Government Performance and Accountability Act of 1994, to enable individuals with developmental disabilities to live everyday lives, as measured by achievement of valued personal outcomes appropriate to life stages from birth to death."*)

	Performance Measures	**Performance Standards**
Outcomes:	Percentage of people who have a quality of life score of 19 out of 25 or greater on the Outcome Based Performance Measures Assessment at annual reassessment	76%
	Percentage of adults living in homes of their own	16.25%
	Percentage of people who are employed in integrated settings	25.50%
	Percentage of clients satisfied with services	95%
Outputs:	Children and adults provided case management	27,829
	Children and adults provided residential care	4,764
	Children and adults provided individualized supports and services	27,829

Source: Florida General Appropriations Act for Fiscal Year 1998–1999.

specific authorizing legislation for the program, available through the statutes on-line on the Florida legislature's web site.

- Program resources. Reports the amount of funding and number of personnel positions authorized in forms ranging from legislative appropriations for the current year to program expenditures for the previous fiscal year.
- Measures of program performance. Reports whether the program has performance-based budget and displays performance measures and other performance information.
- Issues and evaluation. Offers an assessment of the policy issues facing the program in its operating environment and summarizes OPPAGA comments regarding policy issues and program performance that have appeared in other reports.
- Related reports and information. Offers references to other reports, contact persons, and the OPPAGA analyst responsible for the profile. Contains links to the

subject program's web site, other research web sites of interest, and links to OPPAGA evaluation summaries, with full reports available for downloading.

This information is the type of descriptive data that could be included in many paper-published evaluations, but the electronic medium offers unique presentation possibilities. Profiles are technically structured with a document called a *front page*, which contains abbreviated and summary information. This document is linked through hyperlinks embedded in its text to other documents associated with a profile called *back pages*, which offer more detail. This structure allows the user to read as much or as little detail as desired, so that supporting information exists behind a paragraph rather than as part of a paragraph. In contrast, a paper presentation might require that the detail exist on the page or in an appendix that the user would be required to turn to elsewhere in the publication.

The electronic medium also imposes challenges to typical styles of preparing the content of a profile. Writing content for electronic delivery requires an even more concise style than does technical writing for paper, with short paragraphs and lay language. These requirements stem from the varied computing environments of World Wide Web users; many users want pages they can easily read on a comparatively small computer screen. On the other hand, the content advantage that web presentation offers is effectively a live bibliography: profiles take advantage of materials already on the web and offer hyperlinks to summaries and reports themselves rather than repeating conclusions published elsewhere.

Electronic tools allow users to find information more intuitively and flexibly than paper documents allow. FGAR provides tools for searching the data based on topic area, keyword, full text, and specific data elements contained in every profile. For example, the topic area search is designed for a user who has a general interest in a broad policy area of Florida government. Choosing one of thirteen topic areas yields a list of profiles, organized by agency, that address the area of interest (Exhibit 7.2). The choice of the "criminal and juvenile justice" topic area returns a list of sixty-three profiles of programs occurring in twelve agencies ranging from the Department of Corrections to the public school system.

Similarly the full text search function capitalizes on the electronic format; the user may enter any word or phrase and find all documents that contain them. Searching for the word *fish* returns documents on environmental topics and also a document reporting that the Florida Game and Fresh Water Fish Commission will suspend the hunting and fishing licenses of citizens who fail to pay required child support. These examples illustrate an FGAR strength: the power of a structured electronic search extends beyond that of a table of contents or an index for a paper evaluation report.

Contributions of the FGAR Approach

FGAR offers a descriptive context for the policymaking debate, in a form that people can easily access and use. Its electronic design supports easier methods for maintaining current content than paper presentation does, which may foster greater use.

Exhibit 7.2. Topic Area Search Screen

Search Florida Government by Topic

Information on every area of Florida government: the Florida Government Accountability Report lets you find information on topics of interest that cross program or agency lines.

Select a topic area to view a list of all of the profiles of state government programs that address the area. Some profiles are listed under more than one topic.

Topic Areas:

Agriculture
Consumer Protection and Insurance
Criminal and Juvenile Justice
Cultural Affairs
Economic Development and Labor
Education
Governmental Support
Health and Social Services
Intergovernmental and Community Affairs
Judicial
Lottery
Natural Resources and Environment
Transportation and Highway Safety

About 380 profiles are available in the Florida Government Accountability Report: a free source of convenient information on state programs that will tell you how each state program uses Florida's tax dollars.

Source: OPPAGA web site.

Descriptive Context. FGAR adds an important component to the policymaking arena: descriptive information about state programs' purposes, activities, and results. If a legislator is to be informed in the public debate about a state program, an important foundation of the discussion is his or her understanding of the general responsibilities and results of the program. Description has immediate and lasting value for policy discussion and is relevant for any legislator regardless of policy perspective.

Descriptive information is also important because it can be used by legislators with values different from those sometimes represented in evaluation reports. Although legislative researchers often look to statute for criteria for evaluation, the values reflected in the criteria may not reflect those of current legislators who are responding to their constituencies. Legislators may find conclusions derived from applying such criteria to be less relevant for their own policy perspectives than is clear descriptive information that displays whom the program serves, its intended effects, and its actual performance. They may then use this descriptive information and apply to it their own values and criteria in the policy discussion. Although FGAR does summarize the status of evaluation about a program and provide links to research sites of interest, it also places these past evaluations in a current descriptive context. The value of the descriptive context may sometimes be overlooked.

Legislative staff members also benefit from the descriptive information in FGAR, which they can use in their bill analyses and periodic research projects. They may conduct research to address the particular policy perspective of the chair and members of their committees using FGAR's descriptive information while bringing current legislative values to their research work. Staff may also use FGAR for the educational aspect of their work, as committee membership changes and staff help new members to develop a knowledge base in the policy area. Descriptive materials are an essential contribution to this effort.

FGAR's descriptive information is available for citizen use and may promote a more informed citizenry in policy discussions. Most of the comments that we have received via the FGAR site deal with questions or comments that citizens have about government services and the lack of information access that they have found. FGAR provides the descriptive information about Florida state government in a comprehensive and organized format that makes relationships among agencies and state programs more apparent. It also offers paths to find detailed information about services or activities directly from state programs with materials on the web. FGAR has been cited as a public service model in a time when a citizenry that is more engaged with government is becoming visible on the Internet.

Electronic Format. Because FGAR is available on the web with a particular design format, the prospects for its use are greater than would be those of a paper encyclopedia of this volume. Its delivery method and design foster accessibility, information currency, and usability of a large volume of information.

FGAR is more accessible than even legislative library resources, because it is available from every legislative computer via the World Wide Web. Internet access is generally high quality for FGAR's primary audience of legislators and staff. All offices in the Capitol buildings are connected by the local area network to Tallahassee's fiber optic network to the web, and district offices are connected similarly by a wide area network. Thus, FGAR is immediately accessible for research or for response to constituent requests. District staff may find access to such an encyclopedic reference most valuable; their knowledge of state government is likely more limited than that of committee staff because of their comparatively higher turnover rate and their remove from the seat of state government. District staff members have recently begun to refer constituents directly to FGAR to gather the specific information they need.

The currency of FGAR's contents may lead to greater sustained use. Legislative evaluation organizations typically have the concern that paper reports may become dated. Because FGAR is published electronically and each profile stands as a separate publication, its content can be easily updated and the document published back to the web. This process can be quite rapid to keep the research tool current. OPPAGA analysts will review and revise each profile semiannually so that FGAR content is current before the annual legislative session and reflects legislative activity that affects state programs.

FGAR's electronic form allows provision of a large volume of information that is not cumbersome despite its size. Although FGAR is a mass of individual profiles, its electronic format makes the bulk of the compendium invisible. There are over two thousand content documents in FGAR, but the user sees only one screen at a time. On paper FGAR's size would be so daunting as to be unusable. Also a paper format would make it impossible to offer full text searching on specific words of interest, even through a very detailed index. Full text searching allows discovery of information that would be practically impossible to find by leafing through a paper volume of FGAR's size. FGAR's structure facilitates better information provision and increases the likelihood of use.

Current use indicates successful design and information provision. When we established FGAR and improved our existing web site to bring it into greater conformity with the FGAR model, the number of visits to the FGAR site skyrocketed from under fifty monthly to over thirty-four hundred monthly as of July 1998. During the first six and one-half months of its operation, FGAR users viewed an average of five profile pages. The site has received a variety of awards from entities that assess the quality of web sites, ranging from *USA Today*'s feature of FGAR as a Hot Site to the National Conference of State Legislature's presentation of a Notable URL Award. FGAR has been featured in publications oriented toward state legislative activities and good government.

Future Directions for FGAR

We believe that use of FGAR will have an effect on the sorts of evaluation tools that the legislature asks for and uses. As FGAR matures, it will offer two important evaluation tools that may speak clearly to legislative decision makers: accumulated performance data and summary evaluations of the quality of important aspects of state program management.

Accumulated Data. Stored data will allow analysis over time. The FGAR site is backed by a database that manages profile documents and also collects historical data to store for future analysis. For example, resource information is retained and dynamically displayed for five years, but the data set will accumulate indefinitely, making trend analysis possible in the future. Performance measures data are also retained in a database so that future analysis can be done on data generated for measures such as those shown in Exhibit 7.1. If the legislature maintains its commitment to requiring substantive performance measures from agencies for performance-based program budgeting, these FGAR databases showing historical resource allocation and performance will be valuable research tools.

Summary Evaluations. The most significant departure in method of evaluation information delivery is the accountability system rating that appears on selected FGAR profiles. The rating is intended to offer a comment on a program's system for generating and using performance data so that legislators have some assurance of the quality of these data for program management and legislative decision making.

Through review of the literature and our own experience in evaluation, OPPAGA has developed a model for how accountability for program results may be approached. Accountability systems are an important part of public management: they provide a framework to give decision makers reliable information on program performance for effective management and wise public resource allocation. An accountability system has these four key components:

- Program goals and objectives. In order for state programs to direct their resources effectively toward achieving state goals, each program's mission and goals must be clearly defined.
- Valid performance measures and indicators. State programs should have a system in place to measure their performance and effectiveness accurately in attaining their goals.
- Data reliability. Performance measures are meaningless unless they are based on reliable information. Programs should have a process in place to ensure that the legislature and the public can be confident that reported performance data are accurate and reliable.
- Reporting information and results. Program managers should receive regular reports on program performance and use this information to help direct and improve program operations. Performance information should also be shared with the public.

After state programs have operated under performance-based budgets for a year, they become statutorily subject to extensive OPPAGA studies, called program evaluation and justification reviews. Our ratings are based on the evaluation fieldwork that analysts conduct for justification reviews, and they use standard criteria for assessing each of the four elements. Their assessment provides an opinion about each of the key elements shown above. Each element will receive one of these ratings:

Meets expectations. The key element being rated satisfactorily supports the overall system of program accountability.

Needs some modifications. The key element being rated generally supports the overall system of program accountability, but some modifications are necessary.

Needs major modifications. The key element being rated generally does not support the overall system of program accountability, and major modifications are critically necessary.

Exhibit 7.3 shows an application of the rating methodology to the Department of Management Services' Information Technology Program, whose goal is to provide employees with high-performance work tools to

Exhibit 7.3. Application of Accountability Rating

Information Technology Program

Accountability Rating	Meets Expectations	Needs Some Modifications	Needs Major Modifications
Program Purpose & Goals	X		
Performance Measures		X	
Data Reliability		X	
Reporting Information & Use by Management		X	

Summary: The Information Technology Program's purpose and goals are clear and comprehensive. Performance measures do not cover some aspects of the program, such as cost effectiveness and customer satisfaction measures. Two of the three program services do not measure customer satisfaction and one service fails to measure cost effectiveness. The Department of Management Services' Inspector General's Office assesses the reliability of program outcome data but has not assessed output data. Further, program managers do not always correct data reliability programs identified by this internal review. Information on program performance is available to the public and the Legislature through the agency strategic plan and the agency web site. However, managers do not routinely use this performance information to improve the program. For example, managers doubt the usefulness of some performance measures to accurately track and report on all program activities.

Source: Florida Government Accountability Report, Department of Management Services, Information Technology Program.

increase the flow and connectivity of information while reducing the cost of operations.

As of July 1998 we rated thirteen state programs, all the programs for which we have conducted or are conducting justification reviews. We plan to issue accountability system ratings annually. In fiscal year 1998–1999, we anticipate conducting thirteen new ratings and updating the thirteen existing ratings.

The accountability rating is not a rating on program performance. It is instead an opinion on the system of monitoring performance and providing information that state programs use. The rating adds a critical and missing evaluation component on information reliability by commenting on data and measures and the extent to which the program itself depends on this information in program management. Such a tool fits a need of decision makers who must make policy and funding decisions using this information, and its design recognizes the skepticism that legislators display over the accuracy of agencies' performance data. The summary quality of the rating is reflective of the electronic medium in which it is presented and the information needs we perceive legislators to have.

Potential Effects of FGAR. In 1992 Florida voters established an eight-year limit to legislative terms; the first terms expiring under this law end in 2000. Legislators elected under this term limit will have less time for learning about many policy areas, as they likely will work to develop expertise in selected issues. FGAR will offer them a comprehensive reference that they can use to gain knowledge quickly about all the programs and policies that they have to vote on. Also, new legislators suspicious of government programs may prefer to use FGAR as an objective source for descriptive information and a summary of current evaluation in an area rather than depending on state programs for information.

Legislative staff will find that FGAR will ease their tasks of research and constituent assistance. Often their work depends heavily on descriptive materials to educate new committee members and to prepare research reports. Legislative staff may use FGAR to speed their research tasks and bill analyses, and they may perhaps find our longer evaluation work more accessible and useful when it is placed in the descriptive and performance context of profiles. Staff offering constituent assistance will use FGAR to answer questions about government and where services are offered.

Citizens using FGAR will begin to understand how the government is structured and be able to find information on services. They may begin to draw on evaluation information because it is made available to them in a format that makes explicit the linkages between programs and their weaknesses, strengths, and results. Researchers will find that comparative government study is possible as never before, offering an evaluation tool for audiences larger than Florida government or citizens.

Most important for OPPAGA's mission, we hope that FGAR will affect the basis on which legislators and staffs make decisions. Our hope is that FGAR, with its immediate delivery of description and evaluation data, will help policymakers bring more evaluation information into their policy debates.

Ongoing Issues. There are a number of challenges for OPPAGA as we maintain and further develop FGAR. Although we developed and implemented a product with statewide coverage in eighteen months, there are information gaps to be filled. Not all profiles contain the same depth of information, and maintaining and developing information is a resource commitment that OPPAGA must confront. It is important to consider development as a multi-year process that must be flexible because legislative information needs may change. At the same time, OPPAGA must continue its adherence to evaluation standards regardless of the delivery medium for our products; such adherence gives our work the credibility so essential for legislative trust in our analysis.

Accessibility of information on the Internet offers a challenge as well as significant benefits. People may be more likely to take information out of context when it is available on a computer screen than when it is in a paper publication; the temporal quality of Internet information may attract looser usage or interpretation of content than would be made with a printed report. Also, information on web pages may be electronically copied and pasted directly into another document, so that attribution of source may be sketchier than if a quotation of material was taken from printed documents. For example, one legislative staffperson reported that FGAR was very useful because he could copy and paste text directly into a bill analysis, but he did not indicate that this text was credited to its author. As people learn that web delivery of a research product offers the same quality of information that holds the same requirements for use and interpretation, some of these perspectives may change.

Web delivery of information also is exposed to the hazard of hacking, in which a determined user might try to access the server on which information is offered and change or destroy content. FGAR's protections are standard server operating system security and web server security mechanisms. Another significant protection is our use of a stand-alone server with a line to the Internet that is not connected to our network. We copy an identical FGAR site from our network to the Internet server, so our primary data are always protected and a copy is available to the public. These are conservative safeguards that an evaluation organization such as OPPAGA finds necessary to preserve credibility of information.

Despite the challenges, FGAR gives OPPAGA a tremendously far-reaching communication tool. By presenting evaluation information in a format accessible to anyone, we empower legislators, their staffs, and their constituencies to obtain knowledge. If Florida's effort to implement performance-based budgeting continues through the years, legislators will find FGAR's combination of descriptive information and performance indicators increasingly valuable. In the combination of performance indicators and our accountability rating that assesses their quality, we will be building a source of credible information for legislators, the larger evaluation community, and the public. Currently FGAR offers a basket of summarized description and evaluation information with many uses. In the future it will also offer a database of performance information and our assessment of its value. With its flexible design and presence on the World Wide Web, FGAR will continue to mature in its response to legislative information needs.

The Florida Government Accountability Report (FGAR) is available at: www.oppaga.state.fl.us\government

GENA C. WADE is product coordinator for the Florida Legislature's Accountability Report in the Office of Program Policy Analysis and Government Accountability.

*The fact that state legislators belong to an oral culture affects the
evaluation reports written for them. The culture affects both the nature
of the knowledge generated for legislators' use and the nature of the
language used to describe that knowledge.*

The Nature of Knowledge and
Language in the Legislative Arena

Nancy C. Zajano, Shannon S. Lochtefeld

Most decision makers, aside from scholars attempting to determine the truth
of a matter, seek knowledge to determine an appropriate course of action
(Scriven, 1991). This common type of decision making is no different in the
legislative arena. It is merely intensified there. Every year state legislators vote
on hundreds of bills, in committee and on the house or senate floor; each bill
presents one of many possible ways of addressing a given topic. The frequency
and importance of these decisions shape the way legislators request and receive
information. Evaluation reports generated for a legislative audience can differ
from evaluations prepared for other audiences in two ways: the nature of the
knowledge specifically generated for legislators' use and the nature of the language used to describe that knowledge. It is our hope that the work of evaluators outside the legislative arena will have a greater influence on policy
decisions once the knowledge and language needs of legislators are better
understood.

Evaluations conducted in the legislative arena may occasionally serve the
"enlightenment" function, as originally articulated by Carol H. Weiss (1977).
That is, evaluations can help shape the conceptual understanding of a social
problem and encourage legislators to think about an issue differently. In general, however, the focus of legislative evaluators is on particular programs and
policies in order to recommend concrete action to legislators. Because legislators need recommendations for action, legislative evaluators are not seeking
knowledge for its own sake or to add to the cumulative understanding of a

The views expressed in this article are those of the authors and not necessarily those of the
Legislative Office of Education Oversight or the Ohio General Assembly.

social quandary. Instead their reports are intended for the more instrumental use of offering such specific advice as whether to support a line item in the state budget or what to put in an amendment to a pending bill (Larsen, 1981; Young and Comtois, 1979; Weiss, 1977).

It is difficult for those outside the legislative arena to appreciate the demands on legislators' time. Legislators have electoral, constituent, and policy-related demands. They receive stacks of mail each day, as well as frequent visits by lobbyists, constituents, agency personnel, and others. Their committee, constituent, electoral, and session calendars leave little time for thoughtful reflection or reading. Paradoxically legislators must be well informed on hundreds of diverse issues. Consequently evaluators have had to learn how to write reports that can be read or briefed in a few minutes.

A number of authors have chronicled the difficulty of crossing the gap between the "assumptive" worlds of state policymakers and those in academia (Diamond, 1997; Donmoyer, 1996a and 1996b; Hetrick and Van Horn, 1988; Marshall, 1988; McDonnell, 1988). Each group works under a different set of assumptions and norms about what knowledge is valued, when and how it can be produced, and how it must be communicated. Most often academics are not included within the inner circle of policy advisers that legislators turn to when pressed to initiate or respond to an action (Marshall, Mitchell, and Wirt, 1986).

Evaluators in academic settings who wish for their work to be used by legislators are especially caught in this gap. Their work has to meet the expectations of their professional and scientific disciplines; in so doing it is less likely to meet the pragmatic needs of policy audiences. The search for knowledge that can be quickly translated into action and the concise and vivid expression of that knowledge are among the ways legislative evaluators can demonstrate to other evaluators how to "speak truth to power" (Wildavsky, 1979).

Nature of Knowledge

The nature of knowledge generated by legislative evaluators is shaped by the needs of state policymakers for frequent and often immediate decision making. The success of a legislative evaluation office and the reports it generates is often measured by the use made of the information, often in the form of the implementation of the report's recommendations.

While some may argue that "it is a mistake to use implementation as a criterion of merit of an evaluation" (Scriven, 1991, p. 303), others recognize the unique client relationship that exists between legislators and staff evaluators (Brown, 1984). Rigorous, high-quality work is essential to the credibility of legislative evaluators. To be deemed effective, however, evaluation as a legislative tool is judged by its use, most often its instrumental use.

Evaluators working in this setting must give policymakers usable, relevant, and timely information while having confidence that the information is true. They have to be able to balance the need for the rigor of the academy with the need of legislators for conciseness. The legislative evaluator's job is to obtain the information in credible ways, under compressed time lines, and write it in a way that is easily scanned.

Thus the nature of legislative decision making necessarily shapes the evaluation process and the knowledge it produces. The need of legislators for particular types of knowledge affects the topics studied, the methodology used, and the timing of the reports. Legislators need information on what programs and policies deserve their support, information that different players can use to make their case in the give and take of the legislative arena, and information that is timely for both electoral and budget cycles.

Knowledge About Particular Programs and Policies. To serve legislators' need for information they can use, evaluators often focus on existing programs and policies or those that are in place elsewhere and might be tried here. In such cases, legislators want to know if the program works and under what circumstances. What are its costs, requirements for implementation, benefits, drawbacks, and intended consequences? For an existing program, the questions include whether it needs to be improved, replaced, expanded, or abandoned.

A couple of years ago our office was required to study the implementation and impact of Head Start in Ohio. Ohio has invested a great deal of state tax money to expand the federally funded Head Start program. Nationally only 38 percent of eligible children are served by Head Start. With Ohio's governor promoting the goal that every eligible child should be served, state legislators wanted more information on both the implementation and the impact of this popular program. In fact little reliable information has been available to them on such matters as its per-child cost to the state, the feasibility of finding teachers and facilities for continual expansion, and whether recent rapid expansion has affected the quality of the programming offered to children and their families. Furthermore given the federal emphasis on whether Head Start agencies meet all 256 of the Head Start process standards, there was no information available on the impact the agencies were having on children and families.

As a legislative evaluation agency, our study of Head Start focused on these practical questions about the program's implementation and impact. It made recommendations to change the way the state funded the program, decrease the emphasis on expansion and attend to its quality, insist on the collection of impact data through the use of a common instrument to measure children's progress, and give new priority to helping children gain the precursor skills for future literacy. An explicit use of the evaluation report occurred when most of its recommendations were incorporated into the language of the state budget shortly after its release.

Another information need in the legislative arena is whether a particular program can help meet state goals. For example, if improvement of student achievement is the goal, does it make sense to provide funding for all-day kindergarten? If so, should it be provided for all school districts or just those with large proportions of children living in poverty? If we have decided that all students must pass a proficiency test to graduate, is the test fair and appropriate? Should we continue to provide remediation courses at state-supported colleges and universities? Are we paying twice for the same instruction by doing so? These questions are posed by legislators who need to know whether to continue to support an ongoing policy as well as whether to respond to advocates' requests to initiate and fund new programs.

Sometimes legislators need information on the consequences of policies and practices that they have put in place. Given the fast pace, complicated topics, and give and take of making budget and programmatic decisions, the full implications of most decisions cannot be anticipated. Their ripple effects often do not become known until after the legislation is passed or a program is in place. Legislators need to learn about both the intended and unintended consequences from sources perceived as neutral to the enterprise. Legislative evaluators can describe such consequences without being seen as either proponents or opponents of the original idea.

An opportunity to provide information on the unintended consequences of legislative actions came in a request to study the state's system for collecting education data. In the late 1980s the Ohio General Assembly mandated the development of the Education Management Information System (EMIS) to collect comparable information about all school districts and buildings on students, staff, and finances. The system was to allow parents and policymakers to compare the performance and spending of different districts and provide comprehensive information on the operation of schools in Ohio. Sensing unwillingness on the part of the state's Department of Education to initiate such a system, the legislature insisted it be completed in less than two years with minimal funding.

A few years later, as part of a comprehensive review of the system, our office pointed out the consequences of legislators' haste and underfunding on the initial design of the system. This initial design still plagues the EMIS and prevents it from fulfilling legislators' ever-increasing expectations for fast, accurate, and complex information.

Knowledge for the Legislative Give and Take. The give and take of the legislative arena affects the nature of knowledge provided by staff evaluators. The most striking example of this characteristic is the choice of topics that are allowed to be evaluated. As Craft (1979) noted two decades ago, the fact that some agencies and programs are politically powerful while others are politically vulnerable affects the choice of study topics. Our study of the Ohio Veterans' Children's Home, for example, took place only after a change in administration shifted the home's allies out of power. When political tides change, some previously taboo topics become open for staff evaluators' review. Thus, whether "knowledge" is made available at all is subject to the political culture of the legislature.

Another aspect of legislative evaluation is the fact that different players in the arena want different types of knowledge about a program. A legislator who is convinced of the worthiness of a new program may attach an evaluation to the funding request in order to secure votes from fellow legislators. Such a sponsor is usually convinced that any fair evaluation will bring a positive message about the merits of the program. Other legislators are convinced that an existing program is misguided or badly managed and want the evaluation to provide detailed evidence of this fact, as well as recommendations for fixing the program. Such legislators will await the evaluation results and personally see that they get used. As Patton (1997) notes, it is often this personal involvement that determines an evaluation's utilization.

Still other legislators are neutral or uncertain about the worth of a new idea or the effectiveness of a given program and want the evaluation to provide some bottom-line information that is timely and accessible. In the midst of the conflicting knowledge needs of these different players, the staff evaluators must walk the fine line of independence.

While not catering to the knowledge needs of any one player over another, the evaluators must be aware of the issues that need addressing in the political arena. As an example, the Head Start study was conducted in the midst of an ongoing debate on welfare reform in Ohio and the rest of the nation. Acknowledging that new federal rules for welfare recipients would affect the need for child care, our report explicitly dealt with whether Head Start's half-day, part-year program would be feasible for families needing full-day, full-year child care in order to work.

Because of legislators' need for advice on this topic, our report included recommendations and cost projections for funding full-day Head Start as well as for combining Head Start with state-subsidized child care. Although not explicitly requested, we included this information because reporting on Head Start in isolation of welfare reform would not have served the information needs of our "customers."

Timeliness of Knowledge. The usefulness of the knowledge in a legislative evaluation is often directly related to the timing of the report's release. As Craft (1979) advised, "For maximum impact report release should be timed to coincide with maximum legislator interest." Often the maximum interest is during the few months every two years when the state budget is being debated. During these harried weeks, legislators need to make hundreds of decisions on programs about which they have limited knowledge. The testimony they receive from program advocates during budget committee hearings says essentially, "This is a wonderful program; give us more money." Legislators have no way of knowing whether it is a wonderful program. If staff evaluators can give them independent information in time for their votes on particular line items in the budget, the knowledge generated by the report is viewed as valuable.

Conversely sometimes knowledge generated by legislative evaluators needs to sit for awhile before it is seen as useful. A topic might be ripe on one policymaker's agenda but not of interest to others. The knowledge gained from a study may sit on the shelf until other events affect its value. In Ohio, for example, the chair of the Senate Education Committee asked our office to study the "cost of a quality education." Although he was interested in what we learned, the report was basically ignored until four years later when the state's school funding system was declared unconstitutional. With the general assembly given one year to come up with a new solution, both the findings and the methodology of our earlier study became useful to policymakers.

A final aspect of timing and knowledge pertains to the evaluation design itself. In Ohio members of the house of representatives are elected every two years. With term limits, no new senator or representative will be in office more than eight years. If a member is to have an effect on education policy and practice, he or she needs to act quickly. As a result, our office is often asked to provide information about new or existing programs within very brief time periods, whether or not it is reasonable to do so. Often a program's impact cannot be reasonably or accurately assessed for many years. The effect of Head Start on subsequent performance on the state's fourth-grade reading test, for example, takes at least six years to track. Setting up evaluation designs that can provide approximate information in a short time span is an ongoing challenge that is not always resolved successfully.

Legislative evaluation offices typically have months, not years, to complete studies. It is often tempting to narrow the evaluation question to a point where it can be answered in the allotted time. Yet the questions legislators need answered are often complex, requiring evaluators to acquire a deep understanding of many technical and policy issues before a coherent and accurate report can be generated. Legislative evaluators must struggle with conducting a study according to the rigorous standards of the academy while meeting the needs of legislators for timely information. The resulting attempt to "satisfice" may fall short of some ideal but must still provide much-needed information to legislators, who will make decisions with or without it. To accomplish this, often time lines are stretched or fewer data collection methods may be used.

The reality of these constraints makes it important that evaluators caution legislators about the limitations in a report's designs, methods, and findings. When it is better to take the time to explain a complex issue than to provide a quick answer to a simplistic question, evaluators should do so. When it is better to provide no actionable policy options because none are apparent, evaluators should do so.

Nature of Language

There has long been a call for evaluators to tailor the content and form of the evaluation results for their particular audience (Greene, 1988). The characteristics of the legislative audience dictate how evaluation information is best presented. Despite the fact that the legislature is predominantly an oral culture, there is the expectation for a written report that documents the results of a program evaluation or policy analysis.

Given that legislators are called on to act in support of or opposition to a particular idea or program, legislative evaluators are expected to provide advice for such action. When an evaluation report arrives in the office, legislators and

their staff look first for the recommendations. In most instances, policymakers need more than a general description of the topic or the myriad possibilities that surround an issue; they want to know what they should *do* about it.

In addition, to compete with the "stories" legislators are told by lobbyists
and other special interests in this oral culture, the legislative evaluation should
include compelling stories of its own that represent the results of the data.
Often policymakers will hear a convincing story from constituents in support
of a particular program or to argue for a change in policy. The responsibility of
the legislative evaluator is to assess whether such a story exemplifies the program or policy or is only an isolated incident that contradicts the norm. To
counter an unrepresentative story, the evaluation needs its own "engaging narrative" (Greene, 1988, p. 344). Although such a narrative often falls prey to
the need for brevity, often the smallest illustrations can help.

In the study of the Education Management Information System, our office
wished to emphasize the importance of individual student data to the EMIS
and to highlight the legislature's own role in prohibiting the use of such data.
We created a list of policy questions, unanswerable with aggregated data, and
included the list in our report. In the past, legislators have blamed the administration of the system for these unanswerable questions. Linking these questions to legislative actions proved to be very powerful.

To meet the language needs of policymakers in state capitals, legislative
evaluators tend to follow several rules of thumb for the overall format and language style of their reports.

In terms of overall format, the most important rule is brevity. The evaluation report itself may be fewer than ten pages. When the report is longer, it
will always include a summary of three to five pages that can be read in a few
minutes. It is safe to assume that the summary is the only part of the report
that most policymakers will read. The few legislators who originally requested
the study may read the full report or have their staff read it, but they will be
unusual. The report itself becomes support documentation for the ideas
quickly gleaned from reading the summary.

In our office, we use the metaphor of an "elevator ride" as the time
allowed to "get the message" in the report. For this reason, we often summarize the summary itself by writing short sentences in the left margin that can
be scanned. If the readers read just these "pullouts" from the text, they will
have a quick view of what the report is about and a general sense of what we
are recommending. We hope these pullouts will entice them to read more, but
we cannot count on it.

Another general guideline is to start the writing with the recommendations
in mind. This is the opposite of the process used to gather the data. In other
words, the evaluation needs to be conducted without any knowledge of what
the eventual recommendations will be. But the final report itself has to be written with an eye to supporting whatever recommendations have been developed
after the analyses are completed, the findings are determined, and the conclusions are reached. The evaluator has to provide all the needed information for

the reader to understand the conclusions and recommendations. Given that we are aiming for brevity, we try to leave out any information that is not needed to understand the recommendations. In other words, we write considerably less than we know.

In addition to the need for brevity and writing with the recommendations in mind, the language style of legislative reports generally adheres to the following guidelines:

- *Consider each sentence carefully.* Any sentence can be lifted out of context and turned into a newspaper headline. While knowing that you can stand behind every word depends mainly on the quality of the research, it is also a function of the quality of the writing.
- *Say it well and simply.* The goal is to convey a complex message in a simple way without distortion. A reader should never have to read a sentence twice to catch its meaning. This standard requires much rewriting and multiple drafts.
- *Avoid jargon.* Program-specific language creates barriers to understanding. When necessary, carefully define words and concepts that may not be familiar to the audience. Repeat the definitions often enough that the reader does not have to return to earlier pages.
- *Use the active voice. Who* did *what* to *whom?* The active voice conveys all necessary information in the most straightforward and easily interpreted way.
- *Use graphics.* Presenting information graphically accommodates visual learners, reinforces important concepts or data, and can condense pages of written material for the casual reader.
- *Use bullet points.* Bullet points, short paragraphs, and highlighted areas or boxes allow the reader to scan a report without missing important information.
- *Abbreviate the methodology.* Legislators' interest in a study design rarely extends beyond knowing one exists. A brief description of an evaluation's methodology can be written in several paragraphs, with details set out in an appendix.
- *Recognize the importance of subheadings.* Subheadings provide an outline for the reader to follow; they can skip over some information and focus more closely on areas of interest.
- *Avoid value-laden words.* There are some words that due to previous experience or association arouse strong feelings in people. Terminology that was hotly debated over ten years ago, for example, can haunt a program evaluation if it is not properly exorcised.

Application to Other Evaluators

As legislators are pressed to initiate new programs or change existing ones, they need the information contained in evaluation reports beyond those written by legislative staff. As witnesses argue for or against a pending law, they bring evidence for their views from a variety of sources, including evaluation reports written for other audiences. Ultimately any evaluation report could be useful in the legislative arena if it is written in an accessible way.

Legislative aides are often the gatekeepers sitting between busy legislators and those trying to influence them. Aides are responsible for screening unsolicited information to see if it will be useful for a bill or other action a legislator is contemplating. In addition, aides often seek out information, looking to learn about a topic in a few days or a few hours. They have to find the bottom line in a study quickly, highlighting those sentences that tell the story concisely and clearly. In effect they are looking for an "index card" version to share with their bosses.

In this setting, legislative aides are the knowledge brokers sitting between authors of evaluation reports and legislators who might use the information in the report. As Marshall, Mitchell, and Wirt (1986) describe, the aides are in the "near circle" surrounding those who make education policy in each state. Academic researchers are generally out of the picture entirely, identified as among the often-forgotten players in the policy arena.

Legislators and their aides do not readily call on academic researchers because the nature of academic knowledge and language is not intended for quick answers. Academicians seek to add to the accumulation of knowledge about a particular field rather than offer conclusions and recommendations for policy decisions. Their language norms are also very different. Academic writing is cautious, qualified, and probabilistic. It is the language of science. Academic researchers must adhere to the standard of replicability when presenting their methodology. They also provide much more detail about the literature that their study extends. Both of these requirements add great length to their reports, which is unnecessary for a legislative audience and often keeps the reports from being used.

This picture could change, however. Evaluators from all fields could find their reports being used by state policymakers if such reports are written in ways that make them accessible to those who need to find and understand the central message quickly. As more policy decisions devolve to the states, evaluators who can communicate in the assumptive world of state legislators may find that their knowledge can influence these decisions.

References

Brown, J. R. "Legislative Program Evaluation: Defining a Legislative Service and a Profession." *Public Administration Review,* 1984, *44* (3), 258–260.

Craft, R. "Legislative Oversight in the States." *GAO Review,* 1979, *14* (3), 22–26.

Diamond, J. "Kinship with the Stars." *Discover,* 1997, *18,* 44–49.

Donmoyer, R. "This Issue: Talking 'Truth' to Power." *Educational Researcher,* 1996a, *25* (8), 2, 9.

Donmoyer, R. "Introduction: Talking 'Truth' to Power: The Conversation Continues." *Educational Researcher,* 1996b, *26* (3), 2, 14.

Greene, J. C. "Communication of Results and Utilization in Participatory Program Evaluation." *Evaluation and Program Planning,* 1988, *11,* 341–351.

Hetrick, B., and Van Horn, C. E. "Educational Research Information: Meeting the Needs of State Policy Makers." *Theory into Practice,* 1988, 27 (2), 106–110.

Larsen, J. K. "Knowledge Utilization: Current Issues." In R. F. Rich (ed.), *The Knowledge Cycle.* Thousand Oaks, Calif.: Sage, 1981.

Marshall, C. "Bridging the Chasm Between Policymakers and Educators." *Theory into Practice,* 1988, 27 (2), 98–105.

Marshall, C., Mitchell, D., and Wirt, F. "The Context of State-Level Policy Formation." *Educational Evaluation and Policy Analysis,* 1986, 8 (4), 347–378.

McDonnell, L. M. "Can Education Speak to State Policy?" *Theory into Practice,* 1988, 27 (2), 91–97.

Patton, M. Q. *Utilization-Focused Evaluation: The New Century Text* (3rd ed.). Thousand Oaks, Calif.: Sage, 1997.

Scriven, M. *Evaluation Thesaurus* (4th ed.). Thousand Oaks, Calif.: Sage, 1991.

Weiss, C. H. "Introduction." In C. H. Weiss (ed.), *Using Social Research in Public Policy Making.* Lexington, Mass.: Heath, 1977.

Wildavsky, A. *Speaking Truth to Power: The Art and Craft of Policy Analysis.* New Brunswick, N.J.: Transaction Books, 1979.

Young, C. J., and Comtois, J. "Increasing Congressional Utilization of Evaluation." In F. M. Zweig (ed.), *Evaluation in Legislation.* Thousand Oaks, Calif.: Sage, 1979.

NANCY C. ZAJANO *is director of the Legislative Office of Education Oversight of the Ohio General Assembly.*

SHANNON S. LOCHTEFELD *is a program evaluator with the Legislative Office of Education Oversight of the Ohio General Assembly.*

Term limits are likely to shape legislative program evaluation for the next decade. As legislatures turn over more quickly, nonpartisan legislative evaluation offices may play a greater role in the public policy arena. They hold the promise of being a source of institutional memory and credible information for the legislature.

The Impact of Term Limits on Legislative Program Evaluation

Rakesh Mohan, Mary Stutzman

Public dissatisfaction with government; distrust of public officials; shrinking public funds; and increased demand for efficiency, effectiveness, and accountability have challenged business-as-usual in state governments. Limiting terms of state legislators is one way to challenge the status quo in government. Legislators, who appropriate billions of dollars annually, often use evaluation results to support or refute political positions in high-stakes policy debates. Because politics and evaluations are inherently related (Brandl, 1978; Palumbo, 1987), legislative evaluators are bound to experience whatever change is brought on them by term limits. How well they understand the political environment and adapt to the change will determine their effectiveness in terms of credibility and use of their evaluation products by the legislature, the primary client or principal stakeholder (Chelimsky, 1995; Patton, 1997).

The literature on the impact of term limits is sparse. It consists primarily of case studies from California and Maine. A considerable portion of the literature uses either formal questionnaires or interviews to reflect the views of legislators, legislative staff, lobbyists, and others on term limits and the anticipated general impact on the functioning of the legislative process. In particular, a series of articles authored by Hansen (1997a, 1997b, and 1997c) and others in *State Legislatures,* a publication of the National Conference of State Legislatures, and a comprehensive survey conducted by the Council of State Governments (Chi and Leatherby, 1998) provide legislative insights into the actual and perceived impact of term limits. Much of the discussion in the literature on term limits focuses on two issues: higher turnover in state legislatures and the resultant loss of experience and institutional memory. This chapter elaborates on these and other issues as they relate to legislative program evaluation.

NEW DIRECTIONS FOR EVALUATION, no. 81, Spring 1999 © Jossey-Bass Publishers

State Limits on Terms of Legislators

Dissatisfaction with Congress, distrust of career politicians, and concerns with governmental responsiveness gave momentum to the term limit movement during the 1990s. It has been offered as a panacea for problems afflicting the American political system. Term limit proponents generally reflect a populist and Jacksonian view of government that extols the virtues of amateur government and reviles professionalism (Kurfirst, 1996; Carey, 1996). According to reformers, limiting terms of elected officials is a way of "cleaning out the barn."

Advocates for term limits note that, particularly in Congress, senators and representatives make careers out of politics. Professionalism, it is argued, threatens representative democracy; it implies separation between professionals (politicians) and the clients (citizens). In turn, professionalism creates distance and disconnects politicians from the needs of those they represent. Congress was "out of touch" with the citizens. Proponents argue that term limits are a way to close this gap and restore representative democracy. They reason that citizen-legislators would be elected if elected offices were no longer long-term career opportunities. These amateurs, in contrast to the professionals they replace, are uncorrupted by career interests and cognizant of the problems facing most Americans (Carey, 1996; Tabarrok, 1994; Will, 1992).

Limiting legislative terms is a political reform that swept through the states during the first half of the 1990s. This national, grassroots effort targeted elected officials at all levels of government. However, the U.S. Supreme Court decision in *U.S. Term Limits, Inc. v. Thornton* (1995) prohibited the states from limiting the amount of time that congresspersons could serve. States, on the other hand, may impose limits on service for state-elected officials. California and Colorado were the first states, in 1990, to enact term limit restrictions. By 1995 twenty-one states had adopted legislation or amended their constitutions to restrict the length of time and the number of terms that legislators could serve; however, in three of these states—Nebraska, Massachusetts, and Washington—state supreme courts voided term limit provisions (National Conference of State Legislatures, 1998).

State provisions differ in terms of date of impact, years of service allowed, and lifetime service bans. The year that term limits take effect ranges from 1996, in Maine and California, to 2008 in Nevada. The years of service limited in a particular chamber ranges from six to twelve years. Four states—Arkansas, California, Michigan, and Oregon—allow senators to serve longer than representatives before limits take effect. Seven of the term limit states have a lifetime ban on number of years served; other states require breaks in service or limit service within a specified time span (Hansen, 1997b).

Turnover in State Legislatures

Turnover, which refers to the proportion of new members in the legislature, varies among the states and by type of chamber. Senates tend to be more stable than their house counterparts, experiencing lower turnover.

Term limits will change the patterns of tenure in state legislatures, with 35 percent of all state legislators now serving under term limits (Hansen, 1997c). In 1996 California and Maine became the first two states to experience term-limited elections. Term limits prevented 26 of the 151 house members and 4 of the 35 senate members in Maine and 22 of the 80 assembly members in California from running for reelection (National Conference of State Legislatures, 1998).

Term limits will accelerate turnover in 1998 when compared to many states' previous rates. In 1998 five states—Arkansas, California, Colorado, Michigan, and Oregon—will apply term limits to either the house or the senate. The number of legislators ineligible to run in 1998 exceeds the 1996 turnover rate in three of these states. House members ineligible to run in 1998 in Arkansas, Michigan, and Oregon number 50 percent, 61 percent, and 37 percent, respectively. Turnovers in the 1996 elections for these states were 20 percent (Arkansas), 21 percent (Michigan), and 32 percent (Oregon). The 1996 turnover rates included not only those who opted not to run (the counterparts of term limit ineligibles) but also those who were defeated (National Conference of State Legislatures, 1998).

Potential Consequences of Term Limits

Not enough time has yet passed to judge the impact of term limits on the way state legislatures and their staff do business in state capitols throughout the country. However, a wide range of opinions and predictions are being offered, many of them grounded in the arguments made for and against term limits. Some have suggested a power shift from the legislative branch to the executive branch, while others foresee an increased reliance on legislative staff. Each state's political culture and the philosophy behind the term limit movement will be key factors in determining the impact of term limits.

Not everyone agrees that term limits will give rise to "citizen-legislators" acting as "trustees" who promote the general public interest (Cain, 1994). In a national survey of legislators, legislative staff, and lobbyists, more than three-fourths of respondents said that they do not support term limits for state legislators (Chi and Leatherby, 1998). Critics and skeptics of the term limit reform cite a number of undesirable outcomes that may result from limiting tenure of legislators (Chi and Leatherby, 1998; Hansen, 1997a, 1997b; Benjamin and Malbin, 1992; Schrag, 1996):

- Lack of institutional memory
- Increased influence of lobbyists and staff
- Focus on short-term versus long-term policies
- Shift of power to the executive branch
- Weakened legislative oversight over the bureaucracies
- Disruption of leadership (committee and leadership instability)

Term limits will result in less experienced legislators who lack policy knowledge and experience. In turn, critics point out, legislators will be more dependent on information from staff, lobbyists, or executive agencies. Shortening the tenure in office also has consequences for decisions. Term limit legislators act like lame ducks in office. Thus, their behavior may be opportunistic since they will not be around to deal with the long-term consequences of their decisions. These legislators may focus on quick fixes and programs that are popular but have severe long-term repercussions; interest in long-term policy options may diminish (Carey, 1996; Capell, 1996).

In term limit states, the balance of power may shift toward the executive branch of government. Some predict that the oversight role of the legislature will be weakened by term limits. For example, executive agencies, knowing that legislators must leave office at determined times, may simply wait out the legislature. Implementation of policy rests mostly with agencies. Unless legislators act early in their careers or move to the other house, they will not be around to oversee program implementation. Under term limits, committee membership and leadership will change more frequently, possibly resulting in more unstable management and staffing of standing and substantive committees. Policy expertise and institutional memory may be further lost (Carey, 1996; Capell, 1996).

Impact of Term Limits on Legislative Evaluation

The impact of term limits on legislative evaluation promises to be as diverse as the states that have adopted the reform. Term limit states reflect diversity with respect to four key variables that affect and shape the use of evaluation: types of legislatures, party competition, interest group dominance, and organizational context of evaluation offices.

Types of Legislatures. Researchers classify legislatures by the degree of professionalism they exhibit: professional, professional citizen, and citizen legislatures (National Conference of State Legislature, 1994). As Table 9.1 shows, this classification is based on member characteristics (full-time status and pay), staffing (staff size and specialization), and institutional stability (turnover). Term limits stand to change the patterns and composition of the professional legislatures (California, Michigan, and Ohio) the most. In contrast, citizen legislatures, such as those found in South Dakota and Maine, already experience a relatively high degree of turnover and smaller staffs. One would expect less dramatic impacts of term limits in these states as compared to the professional legislatures.

Party Competition. The competition between the two political parties for controlling legislative chambers as well as the state's top executive office is another key variable that influences how legislative evaluation will be structured and used as term limits begin. The demand for nonpartisan information is likely to increase in those states where competition between Democrats and Republicans within a chamber or between chambers is high.

Table 9.1. Key Variables Affecting Evaluation Entities in Term Limit States

Term Limit States	Evaluation Entity (and the Governing Body)	Type of Legislature	Party Competition	Interset Group Dominance
Arizona	Office of the Auditor General (Joint Audit Committee)	PC	Competitive-LR	Mixed
Arkansas	Division of Legislative Audit (Joint Audit Committee)	C	Traditional-DA	Mixed
California	Bureau of State Audits (Joint Audit Committee)	P	Competitive-LD	Mixed
Colorado	Colorado State Auditor's Office (Joint Audit Committee)	PC	Competitive-LR	Complementary
Florida	Office of Program Policy Analysis and Government Accountability (Joint Audit Committee)	PC	Traditional-DA (Growing RS)	Dominant
	Office of the Auditor General (Joint Audit Committee)			
Idaho	Office of Performance Evaluations (Joint Oversight Committee)	C	Competitive-LR	Mixed
Louisiana	Office of the Legislative Auditor (Joint Audit Committee)	PC	Traditional-DA	Dominant
Maine	Office of Policy and Legal Analysis (Legislative Council)	C	Competitive-LD	Complementary
Michigan	Office of the Auditor General (Constitutional Provision)	P	Competitive-LD	Complementary
Missouri	Oversight Division (Joint Legislative Research)	PC	Traditional-DA	Complementary
Montana	Office of the Legislative Auditor (Joint Audit Committee)	C	Competitive-LD	Mixed
Nevada	Legislative Counsel Bureau (Joint Legislative Council)	C	Traditional-DA	Dominant
Ohio	Legislative Office of Education Oversight (Joint Committee on Education Oversight)	P	Competitive-LD	Mixed
	Legislative Service Commission (Joint Legislative Commission)			
Oklahoma	House Fiscal Staff (House Appropriations and Budget Committee)	PC	Traditional-DA (Growing RS)	Mixed
Oregon	Legislative Fiscal Office (Joint Legislative Audit Committee)	PC	Competitive-LD	Mixed
	State Audits Division (Secretary of State)			
South Dakota	Legislative Audit (Joint Legislative Council)	C	Traditional-RA	Mixed
	Legislative Research Council (Joint Legislative Council)			
Utah	Office of the Legislative Auditor (Joint Legislative Management Committee)	C	Competitive-LR	Complementary
Wyoming	Legislative Service Office (Joint Management Audit Committee)	C	Competitive-LR	Mixed

Note: P = professional, C = citizen, PC = professional citizen, DA = Democratic advantage, RA = Republican advantage, RS = Republican strength, LD = leaning Democratic, LR = leaning Republican.

Sources: Dye (1997); National Conference of State Legislatures (1994); Thomas and Hrebenar (1996).

Party competition varies considerably among the term limit states (listed in Table 9.1). Based on percentage of times between 1968 and 1994 that Democrats or Republicans controlled the governorship and both houses of the state legislature, Dye (1997) classifies states into five groups: traditional with Democratic advantage, traditional Democratic but growing Republican strength, competitive leaning Democratic, competitive leaning Republican, and traditional with Republican advantage. As Table 9.1 shows, eleven of the eighteen term limit states are classified as competitive. In addition, two traditionally Democratic states, Florida and Oklahoma, have displayed growing Republican strength. Since legislative evaluation can provide a more neutral source of program information, legislative evaluation activities and products may increase in these competitive party states when term limits become effective.

Interest Groups Dominance. Another factor that can affect legislative evaluation as term limits kick in is the role of interest groups in a particular state. If interest groups become more dominant in providing information to novice and less experienced legislators, there may be outcries to expand the capacity within the legislatures themselves to produce more independent and nonpartisan information. Interest group influence in a state is the extent to which interest groups as a whole influence public policy as compared to other players in the political system (such as political parties, the legislature, and the executive branch).

Thomas and Hrebenar (1996) provide a classification of interest group influence. Using this approach, states are classified as having a dominant, complementary, or subordinate interest group system regarding policy impact relative to the parties and other branches of government (see Table 9.1). In a majority of term limit states, interest group influence on public policy is a mixture of dominance and complementary to other entities; only in South Dakota is the interest group influence characterized as a mixture that is complementary and subordinate to other entities. Interest groups are characterized as dominant in three states: Florida, Louisiana, and Nevada. Complementary interest group systems are found in Colorado, Maine, Michigan, Missouri, and Utah.

Organizational Context of Evaluation Offices. Traditionally legislative evaluation assumed a major role in government as that of watchdog of public funds and programs. Many states established audit organizations that focused primarily on program economy, efficiency, effectiveness, and legal compliance in state government. As Brooks (1996) notes, the divisions between traditional auditing and program evaluations are declining. Both audit perspectives and more traditional evaluation approaches can now be found in the states. The approaches and methods used by the two are blended in state legislative evaluation activities.

Although all of the eighteen states embarking on term limits currently have nonpartisan evaluation entities, no two states conduct evaluations in the same way (Mohan, 1997). Each evaluation organization belonging to the National Legislative Program Evaluation Society (NLPES) is nonpartisan and organizationally independent from the programs and agencies it evaluates. These evaluation organizations typically report to a joint legislative oversight committee that includes members from both chambers of the legislature (see

Table 9.1). In addition to the joint committees, some of these organizations report to budget or standing committees. To keep evaluation organizations independent and insulated from individual legislators, requests for specific studies and analyses are generally processed through joint committees that assign and approve studies. In addition to the joint committees, evaluation organizations receive work assignments through statutory provisions, as well as independently identifying areas of study.

There is a great deal of variability among the states in terms of what constitutes evaluation, with activities ranging from reporting on compliance with laws to performing sophisticated analyses of public policy. Audit organizations tend to emphasize program audits, while other evaluation offices tend to perform more general evaluation activities. Legislative evaluation entities produce a wide array of products (Mohan, 1997):

- Program audits (performance and compliance)
- Program evaluations (summative and formative evaluations, policy analyses, implementation analyses, and performance monitoring)
- Other products and activities (best-practice reviews, performance and accountability measurement, and sunset reviews)

Responding to Changes: Future Trends for Legislative Evaluation

Legislative staffs, including evaluation units, have evolved and changed to meet new challenges (Weberg, 1997). Term limits promise to be another environmental change that will shape legislative evaluation for the next decade. The impact of term limits will not be the same throughout the states; the way these organizations meet the challenges posed by leadership turnover and growing inexperience of legislative members will be as varied as the states themselves. As legislatures turn over more quickly, nonpartisan evaluation shops hold the promise of being a source of institutional memory and producer of credible information for the legislature as a whole. For legislative evaluation units to produce credible and useful information and maintain a presence in the legislative arena, changes may occur in terms of evaluation products and relationship with stakeholders (see Figure 9.1).

Evaluation Products. The type of evaluation studies will change in term limit states. To meet the problems associated with the lack of institutional memories, audit reports and evaluations will need to include more background and contextual information. In addition, policy syntheses and meta-analyses may be a useful way in which some organizations attempt to meet the needs of members. The length of time to conduct studies will probably be shortened. Term-limited legislators want information during their tenure in office; thus, the emphasis on short-term studies versus long-range analyses may increase.

Relationship with Stakeholders. The success of legislative program evaluation in term limit states rests with paying attention to stakeholder

Figure 9.1. Schematic Showing the Impact of Term Limits on Legislative Program Evaluation

Legislative Evaluation Environment

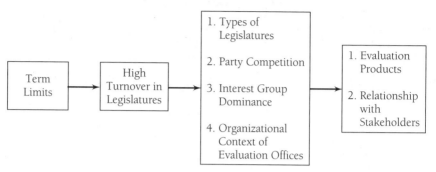

changes and making explicit efforts to assess the potential use of their products. As legislatures turn over more quickly, this role is likely to change to include an additional dimension: nonpartisan evaluation offices have the promise of being a source of institutional memory or continuity for the legislature as a whole. In addition to serving as evaluators, they may be asked to educate the new members of the legislature by providing background information on policy issues under consideration.

Since term limits promote turnover, familiarity with legislative evaluation may decline. Thus, evaluation organizations will need to market themselves and their services. This may take the form of conducting workshops explaining evaluation or providing short briefing papers and materials about their offices. To facilitate instrumental use of their reports and studies, timeliness of release will be imperative. Perhaps one of the challenges will be cultivating and maintaining sources of support for evaluations. This is particularly true for studies that were either requested by lame ducks or the reasons for requesting the study have been long forgotten. The number of legislative evaluation units within a state may increase, which could conceivably attach or expand program evaluation functions to substantive policy committees such as natural resources or education. This would be a way of increasing policy knowledge and dealing with problems of bringing members up to speed.

Views from the States. Officials of four legislative evaluation offices in three states—California, Colorado, and Oregon—were contacted in order to learn about their views concerning the impact of term limits on legislative program evaluation. These are three of the six states where term limits went into effect in 1996 and 1998. Term limits in the remaining twelve states will go into effect in the year 2000 or after. As expected, each of the four offices has experienced the term limit phenomenon differently (Table 9.2). However, there were shared views on two issues:

Table 9.2. Comments on the Impact of Term Limits by Legislative Evaluation Officals in California, Colorado, and Oregon

Evaluation office 1

- Term limits have not had any impact on the evaluation work and products.
- Term limits have had an effect on institutional knowledge. The office spends more time educating new legislators about the office and its products. This includes preparing summaries of audits for various budget subcommittees.
- Often experienced staff members working for senior legislators leave the legislature when their legislators leave. Therefore, the office has to do more educating of new, less experienced staff members.
- Two senior members of the joint legislative audit committee have been termed out. They worked on the committee for many years.
- The office has not seen the full impact of term limits yet.

Evaluation office 2

- The office had not seen any discernible impact and does not anticipate a significant change with respect to types of assignments, study topics, and reports.
- Because of term limits, the Joint Legislative Audit Committee will lose its current chair, who has been a member of the committee for a long time.
- A number of legislators affected by term limits are planning to run for the different chamber.

Evaluation office 3

- The biggest change the office has seen so far is that the office does more educating about various state programs. Reports now go into more explanation and history of the program.
- Because of the lack of institutional memory and experience about various programs in the legislature, the office would need to be more aware of possible areas of reviews and suggest those areas to legislators for their consideration and approval.

Evaluation office 4

- Changes have more to do with the whole political climate, including term limits and increased demand for accountability, efficiency, and effectiveness.
- Generally new legislators have very little understanding for the audit process and audit standards. For example, reports need to explain controls and risks in a way that legislators can easily understand.
- The office needs to do more topical studies and produce timely reports.

Note: Oregon has two offices that conduct evaluations for the legislature. One of the offices, the Oregon State Audits Division, is under the secretary of state. However, it works closely with the Joint Legislative Audit Committee.

Source: Telephone interviews with management officials of legislative evaluation offices. To maintain the anonymity of the offices and respondents, names of the states, offices, and officials are not mentioned.

- Legislative evaluation offices need to increase their efforts in educating legislators.
- The full impact of term limits is not yet known.

Conclusion

Term limits promise to change the state landscape throughout the next decade. This reform poses challenges and offers new opportunities to legislative evaluation entities currently in place; it may also stimulate the creation of additional organizations within the legislature and new types of products to help fill gaps of lost institutional memory and less experienced legislative members. Legislative program evaluators have risen to challenges posed in their environment in the past; they will adapt and continue to modify their organizations and products. The contours and changes in legislative evaluation are now just beginning to unfold.

References

Benjamin, G., and Malbin, M. J. (eds.). *Limiting Legislative Terms.* Washington, D.C.: Congressional Quarterly, 1992.

Brandl, J. E. "Evaluation and Politics." *Evaluation,* 1978, Special Issue, 6–7.

Brooks, R. A. *Blending Two Cultures: State Legislative Auditing and Evaluation.* New Directions for Evaluation, no. 71. San Francisco: Jossey-Bass, 1996.

Cain, B. "Term Limits: Not the Answer to What Ails Politics." In E. H. Crane and R. Pilon (eds.), *The Politics and Law of Term Limits.* Washington, D.C.: Cato Institute, 1994.

Capell, E. A. "The Impact on Term Limits on the California Legislature: An Interest Group Perspective." In Bernard Grofman (ed.), *Legislative Term Limits: Public Choice Perspectives.* Boston: Kluwer, 1996.

Carey, J. M. *Term Limits and Legislative Representation.* New York: Cambridge University Press, 1996.

Chelimsky, E. "The Political Environment of Evaluation and What It Means for the Development of the Field." *Evaluation Practice,* 1995, *16* (3), 215–225.

Chi, K. S., and Leatherby, D. "State Legislative Term Limits." *Solutions,* Feb. 1998.

Dye, T. R. *Politics in States and Communities.* Upper Saddle River, N.J.: Prentice Hall, 1997.

Hansen, K. "The Third Revolution." *State Legislatures,* 1997a, *23* (8), 20–26.

Hansen, K. "Term Limits for Better or Worse." *State Legislatures,* 1997b, *23* (7), 50–57.

Hansen, K. "Living Within the Limits." *State Legislatures,* 1997c, *23* (6), 13–19.

Kurfirst, R. "Term-Limit Logic: Paradigms and Paradoxes." *Polity,* Fall 1996, pp. 119–140.

Mohan, R. "Legislative Evaluators: A Diverse Group of Professionals." In National Conference of State Legislatures' *NLPES News,* May 1997.

National Conference of State Legislatures. NCSLnet: State Term Limit Provisions. Website (www.ncsl.org), July 17, 1998.

National Conference of State Legislatures. "A Second Look at the Cost of Legislatures." *State Legislatures,* 1994, *20* (11), 5.

Palumbo, D. J. (ed.). *The Politics of Program Evaluation.* Thousand Oaks, Calif.: Sage, 1987.

Patton, M. Q. *Utilization-Focused Evaluation: The New Century Text.* Thousand Oaks, Calif.: Sage, 1997.

Schrag, P. "The Populist Road to Hell: Term Limits in California." *American Prospect,* Winter 1996, pp. 24–30.

Tabarrok, A. "A Survey, Critique and New Defense of Term Limits." *Cato Journal*, 1994, *14* (2), 333–350.

Thomas, C., and Hrebenar, R. J. "Interest Groups in the States." In V. Gray and H. Jacob (eds.), *Politics in the American States*. Washington, D.C.: CQ Press, 1996.

Weberg, B. "New Age Dawns for Legislative Staff." *State Legislatures*, 1997, *23* (1), 26–31.

Will, G. *Restoration: Congress, Term Limits, and the Recovery of Deliberative Democracy*. New York: Free Press, 1992.

RAKESH MOHAN is a principal management auditor for the Washington State Joint Legislative Audit and Review Committee.

MARY STUTZMAN is a methodologist for the Florida Office of Program Policy Analysis and Government Accountability.

INDEX

Back Issue/Subscription Order Form

Copy or detach and send to:
Jossey-Bass Inc., Publishers, 350 Sansome Street, San Francisco CA 94104-1342

Call or fax toll free!
Phone 888-378-2537 6AM-5PM PST; Fax 800-605-2665

Back issues: Please send me the following issues at $23 each.
(Important: please include series initials and issue number, such as EV90.)

1. EV _____

_____

_____

$ _____ Total for single issues

$ _____ Shipping charges (for single issues *only;* subscriptions are exempt from shipping charges): Up to $30, add $5^{50} • $30^{01}–$50, add $6^{50} $50^{01}–$75, add $7^{50} • $75^{01}–$100, add $9 • $100^{01}–$150, add $10 Over $150, call for shipping charge.

Subscriptions   Please ❏ start   ❏ renew my subscription to *New Directions for Evaluation* for the year 19___ at the following rate:

❏ Individual $65   ❏ Institutional $115
NOTE: Subscriptions are quarterly, and are for the calendar year only. Subscriptions begin with the spring issue of the year indicated above. For shipping outside the U.S., please add $25.

$ _____ Total single issues and subscriptions (CA, IN, NJ, NY and DC residents, add sales tax for single issues. NY and DC residents must include shipping charges when calculating sales tax. NY and Canadian residents only, add sales tax for subscriptions.)

❏ Payment enclosed (U.S. check or money order only)
❏ VISA, MC, AmEx, Discover Card #_____ Exp. date_____

Signature _____ Day phone _____
❏ Bill me (U.S. institutional orders only. Purchase order required.)
Purchase order #_____

Name _____
Address _____

_____

Phone_____ E-mail _____

For more information about Jossey-Bass Publishers, visit our Web site at:
www.josseybass.com   **PRIORITY CODE = ND1**